1 MONTH OF
FREE
READING

at
www.ForgottenBooks.com

By purchasing this book you are eligible for one month membership to ForgottenBooks.com, giving you unlimited access to our entire collection of over 1,000,000 titles via our web site and mobile apps.

To claim your free month visit:
www.forgottenbooks.com/free915332

* Offer is valid for 45 days from date of purchase. Terms and conditions apply.

ISBN 978-0-266-95652-5
PIBN 10915332

This book is a reproduction of an important historical work. Forgotten Books uses
state-of-the-art technology to digitally reconstruct the work, preserving the original format
whilst repairing imperfections present in the aged copy. In rare cases, an imperfection in
the original, such as a blemish or missing page, may be replicated in our edition. We do,
however, repair the vast majority of imperfections successfully; any imperfections that
remain are intentionally left to preserve the state of such historical works.

Forgotten Books is a registered trademark of FB &c Ltd.
Copyright © 2018 FB &c Ltd.
FB &c Ltd, Dalton House, 60 Windsor Avenue, London, SW19 2RR.
Company number 08720141. Registered in England and Wales.

For support please visit www.forgottenbooks.com

TWEEDS FOR COLLEGE MEN

There is no more comfortable garment for winter wear than one of the new herringbone tweeds in a lounge drape model.

The Earl has a three-button jacket, notch lapels rolled to the middle button, and tapered trousers. Its soft lounge effect is typical of garments worn by the well-turned-out college man.

Tweeds from $32.50

Ed Provan

275 YONGE STREET (Between the Imperial & Childs) TORONTO

COMPLIMENTS
OF

THE
F. P. WEAVER COAL CO.
LIMITED

●

IMPORTERS AND WHOLESALERS

OF

DOMESTIC AND INDUSTRIAL

COALS

●

347 BAY STREET   TORONTO

ELGIN 3271

St. Andrew's College Review

CAMP KAGAWONG

AFFILIATED WITH ST. ANDREW'S COLLEGE FOR THE PAST 31 YEARS

For fully illustrated booklet and further information apply

E. A. CHAPMAN, 143 ALEXANDRA BLVD., TORONTO

Gentlemen prefer SIGNET RINGS as Christmas GIFTS

A. Natural 10 kt. gold Signet Ring - - - - - $5.00

B. Green gold with white top, 10 kt. - - - - - $8.50

C. Bloodstone Signet Ring, 10 kt. natural gold - $13.50

D. Bloodstone Signet Ring, with fluted shoulders, natural 10 kt. gold - - - - $20.00

BIRKS-ELLIS-RYRIE

Yonge at Temperance - Toronto

IF you want good printing together with service and co-operation;

IF convenience of location, experience and a desire to give satisfaction are important factors;

IF cost is a vital consideration provided quality is not sacrificed

THEN consult your own University Press for further information.

◆

THE UNIVERSITY OF TORONTO PRESS
TORONTO, CANADA

"Syl" Apps

Dynamic Young Centre Ice Star
of the Toronto Maple Leafs

Endorses This

SKATE OUTFIT

exclusively for

Simpson's

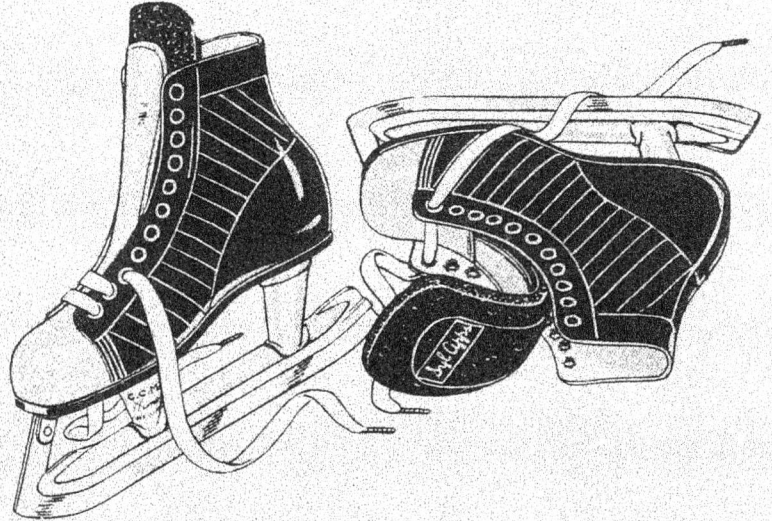

Here's a skate outfit that's approved by one of the greatest young players in the N.H.L. today—for the "greats" of tomorrow! Designed with the latest pro features—shoe is made of chrome side English kip, with leather lining, solid leather insole and outsole, solid leather block toe with tan tip, and leather tongue with felt lining; correctly attached to a C.C.M. aluminum-finished hockey tube skate with high-carbon steel blade. Boys' sizes 1 to 5; men's sizes 6 to 12. Only at Simpson's—write Shopping Service. Outfit, 4.95.

Simpson's Sporting Goods—Fourth Floor

CONTENTS

Editorial	13
Mrs. Macdonald	16
Contributors, and Literary Efforts	
By Flemming	19
By Wilson	20
A Hundred Years Ago	22
If Only Fiction Were Truth	23
Stanley Comes Across	24
The Naval Review	25
All that Glitters is not Gold	26
Sitting on the Back Bridge, November, 1937	28
Dr. Kilpatrick's Sermon	29
Our College	39
Far Across the Waters	64
School News	
Prize Day	33
Beagle Hunt, Mr. Finlay, Camera Club	34
Ping-Pong, Football Dinner	35
Chapel Notes	37
Games and Sports	
Football	40
Rugby Sevens, Soccer Sixes	60
Cross Country Run, Swimming	61
Basketball	63
Macdonald House, Editorial	65
Football	68
Cross Country Run	76
Contributors' Pages	
The Changing of the Colours	73
Motherly Care	75
Old Boys' News	81
Exchanges	90

St. Andrew's College
Aurora, Ontario

ADVISORY BOARD

His Grace, The Duke of Devonshire, K.G.
Col. Thomas Cantley, M.P., LL.D., New Glasgow, N.S.
Sir Edward Beatty, LL.D., Montreal, Que.
Sir Robert Falconer, K.C.M.G., D.Litt., Toronto

BOARD OF GOVERNORS

Chairman, Sir Joseph Flavelle, Bart., LL.D

Whiteford G. Bell, Esq.
Graham Campbell, Esq.
Gordon T. Cassels, Esq.
The Hon. and Rev. H. J. Cody, M.A., D.D., LL.D.
D. Moffat Dunlap, Esq.
Duncan Graham, M.B., F.R.C.P.
Charles D. Gossage, M.D., F.R.C.S.
R. E. Grass, Esq., K.C.
D. B. Hanna, Esq.
H. B. Housser, Esq.
The Headmaster
Rev. G. G. D. Kilpatrick, M.A., D.D.
W. B. McPherson, Esq., K.C.
Rev. D. Bruce Macdonald, M.A., LL.D.
Lt.-Col. J. F. Michie
Lorne C. Montgomery, M.D., C.M., F.R.C.P.
T. A. Russell, Esq., LL.D.
Rev. J. R. P. Sclater, M.A., D.D.

Graham F. Towers, Esq.

Gordon W. Hewitt, Esq.
R. C. Kilgour, Esq., Sr.
Percy D. McAvity, Esq.
} *Representing the Old Boys' Association*

Secretary of the Board

W. A. Beer, Esq.

The St. Andrew's College Review

Christmas 1937

Editor—K. E. Rogers

Editorial Board

H. E. Archibald
J. F. Macdonald I
M. T. Wilson
D. Kilpatrick
D. McLelland I
J. Farrer

J. A. O'Brian I
A. S. Cockfield
M. S. Kent
O. Morlock
J. Macdonald II

Lower School Editor—J. Kilpatrick II

Staff Adviser—Mr. G. S. O'Brian

"A Merry Christmas, Bob" said Scrooge, with an earnestness that could not be mistaken, as he clapped him on the back. "A Merrier Christmas, Bob, my good fellow, than I have given you for many a year. I'll raise your salary, and endeavor to assist your struggling family, and we will discuss your affairs this very afternoon over a Christmas bowl of smoking bishop, Bob! Make up the fires, and buy another coal-scuttle before you dot another i; Bob Cratchit!"

Scrooge was better than his word. He did it all, and infinitely more; and to Tiny Tim, who did NOT die, he was a second father

BLESS CHARLES DICKENS and Scrooge, and all Scrooges and Tiny Tims! A world that cannot be saved by thought, may yet be saved by laughter. So let us laugh! Let us pretend we are the Scrooge come right,—as he did in the end. That is quite enough for us all—whether we are going home, or to somebody else's home, or whether we are going to rally round the fire at old St. Andrew's. Away with books and class-room bells! Bring on tinsel, and tissue-paper, and church bells and a frosty morning. May there be laughter and stamping of feet and snow brought in on the boots. "Rejoice and be exceeding glad, for unto us a Saviour is given."

MRS. MACDONALD

St. Andrew's College Review

Christmas, 1937

THROUGHOUT this term, time's ruthless hand has been ever moving in front of us—or behind us, pressing into ten short weeks everything that is usually done in thirteen. Perhaps we have taken old Father Time firmly by the forelock this autumn; in any case, the term has been a good one. All the reflected sides of our corporate life,—knowledge, games and the big intangible Andrean background seem somehow to have strode on bravely and well.

* * *

The school was greatly shocked to hear of the sudden death of Mrs. Macdonald early in the term. She was a living part of the College for many years. Our loss is expressed by Dr. Robinson elsewhere in this issue.

* * *

With the beginning of this term a new system was instituted which isolated the boys in each house more than they have been in the past. This new scheme soon began to show its value by increasing the standing of the senior boys in Memorial House. The boys coming up from Lower School and new boys in Flavelle House now realize that it is more than a few weeks before they can be classed as senior boys. The boys in Flavelle House are now referred to as the "Middle School" while the boys in Memorial House are referred to as the "Upper School". The Upper School's privileges include 10.30 p.m. "lights".

"You may give up battling hard during the game fellows—likely you will be the only one who knows it but, it is only yourself whom you are letting down." Everyone on the first rugby squad knows who was speaking—Bobby Porter—the coach. Bob has been more than a coach to the team; he soon became a firm friend welcomed by all with open arms. We have been practically assured of his return next year as coach, and those of us who are leaving at the end of this year feel sure the spirit he has started will continue to grow and spread. We are very grateful to Mr. Joe Breen, also, who during the season attended some of our practices, giving very helpful hints where and when needed.

In another section of this issue we record the games played, and say a covering word or two. We are not particularly jubilant when we record one win and four losses; yet nobody beat the team very badly; we always seemed to have a chance, and in every game were playing harder when the final whistle blew. Our line was good, our backfield inexperienced, and we had no really good kicker. (I think that's the story.) We always have the full range of next season to turn our thoughts to, although we are uncertain of who is coming back.

* * *

The REVIEW takes much pleasure on behalf of the boys in welcoming Mr. Kenneth Ives, formerly of St. George's School, Vancouver, to the staff. Mr. Ives graduated from the University of Alberta with a B.A. degree and from Toronto University with an M.A. degree.

* * *

One of the many results of the late opening has been the delaying of Cadet Corps training until the Summer term. This year Mr. O'Brian will fill the place vacated by Mr. Dowden. In the meantime we miss (?) the sweet discordant skirling of the bag-pipes and the "Form, fours!—one! one-two!" on the quadrangle every morning.

* * *

Early in November Mrs. Ketchum entered the Toronto General Hospital to undergo a serious operation. It was with much pleasure that the school heard she was soon on the road to recovery.

* * *

Early in the term the Headmaster appointed the following prefects: Bonnell, Christie, Macdonald I, O'Brian I and Rogers.

* * *

This year the Lower School made a stride or two in the right direction. They have, first, their own dining-room operating. Instead of having to hurry over to the Upper School in all weathers, Lower School boys now grace their own tables thereby gaining a few more minutes in which to eat. In the second place three line playing fields, two rugby and one soccer, have been laid out for them west of the school buildings. There is now plenty of room for every boy in the school to play football on some squad. The seven football fields were all busily used every day this season.

* * *

I think we mentioned Father Time earlier in our so-called Editorial. Near the end of our effort we feel less sure that we are holding that forelock of his as firmly as we boasted. Classroom work is bearing down. The masters seem to be determined in their idea of making up for lost time. One master said in class that there were only fifteen days left till the end of the term; the class started to cheer. It must be remembered always that there are two points of view. As far as your editor is aware, classwork in the school is in good shape.

* * *

Whenever an issue of the REVIEW looms imminent we say, "Last number was good, this one looks like a flop." Flop or not, we extend thanks to all our contributors. The Editorial staff is completely in your hands for material, and cannot make bricks without straw! REVIEW pages cost money, and much good material has been returned with thanks because it was found impossible to print it all.

* * *

To-night your editor is sitting up with the thought that the printer goes to work in the morning. Outside, the snow is falling heavily. Harry Davis is "puddling-in" the rinks. There are a couple of toboggans and one pair of skis lying out on the quad where the dinner bell to-night caught unawares the Lower School boys doing winter sports behind the Head's house. Good old winter. Now the old street-lamps around the quad have been switched off. But it's still snowing.

A Merry Christmas, Everybody.
K.E.R.

Mrs. Macdonald

IT was in January, 1901, that Mrs. Macdonald came as a bride to St. Andrew's College, and immediately by her gaiety, her ready sympathy, her youthful charm and dignity won the affection and respect of all with whom she was associated. Chestnut Park, the first home of the School, was a building rapidly falling into decay; the radiant youth of its new mistress imparted a fresh atmosphere of optimism and enthusiasm to the rambling and gloomy old mansion. In a small apartment surrounded on all sides by the boys Dr. and Mrs. Macdonald began their married life, dispensing a generous hospitality at all hours of the day and night to schoolboys and their parents and to the various members of the staff. It was not long before the boys discovered that in the Headmaster's wife they had a friend with whom they could discuss all their problems and ambitions.

The School grew rapidly. At the end of six years it became necessary to remove to a large and commodious building in North Rosedale; and here the happy life of the School in which Mrs. Macdonald so greatly rejoiced continued with many triumphs and successes down to the Great War. She took the keenest interest in all that went on in the School; in the School matches, in the Cadet Corps dances and in the entertainments of the Literary Society in which her fondness for the drama enabled her to give valuable assistance. When the calamities of the Great War came it is not surprising that they brought heavy sorrows to one who followed with a maternal solicitude and affection the careers of those who had spent their school days at St. Andrew's, so many of whom were destined to suffer in France; the death of each came with the shock of personal grief and those tragic years when so many bright and promising lives went out made serious inroads into a constitution never at any time robust. Many letters from the trenches bear witness to the affection of old Andreans and their appreciation of the comforts which were sent to them under her direction.

In the last year of the war the building in Rosedale was taken over by the Government as a hospital and St. Andrew's moved to Knox College on the University campus. Here for the next two years the School prospered greatly, but the strain of these and two subsequent movings greatly impaired Mrs. Macdonald's health. By the time St. Andrew's was established in its present buildings the School had moved four times.

Happy at length in a permanent and settled abode in Aurora the School became aware with deep regret that the health of her to whom its welfare had meant so much was seriously impaired. She had given much. Possessed of artistic gifts of a high order she added charm to everything she touched: much of the beauty of grounds and buildings at Aurora which has so justly been admired is due to her interest and forethought; nothing was too small to escape attention; the many pleasing details of the chapel which has proved so great an addition to the School are of her devising; it was her wish that the windows should be of clear glass and that they should be low enough to command the view over the playing-helds and the surrounding country. Had her wishes been carried out the windows in the class-rooms would also have commanded the many noble views with which the School is surrounded; she was a lover of nature and of far horizons.

And she was a lover of animals. In the days when she became very much of an invalid the devotion of her dogs was very touching; they sometimes made it difficult for her friends to approach.

In her intercourse with the boys she encouraged heroism and endurance and adventure, and discouraged the merely sentimental. She had learned in bearing suffering that much that is good comes through pain; and of this she had her full share. Twenty times either for surgical or medical treatment she entered the hospital and yet her spirit was not broken. To the end she continued to plan and to pray for the prosperity of the School.

On Saturday evening, the 16th of October, she passed quietly and peacefully into unconsciousness, and early Wednesday morning, October 20th, succumbed to pneumonia.

A few extracts from the many tributes to Mrs. Macdonald will help Andreans of a later day to appreciate the affection in which she was held. ... "It seems like only yesterday, yet it was in the early Fal lof 1913 that Mrs. Macdonald gathered a number of home-sick and more or less frightened kids in the Lower School and entertained them in a most motherly fashion for an entire evening at your residence. I recall being one of that group who seemed to be particularly home-sick, but as the night passed by I decided that after all things were not as black as they looked and St. Andrew's wasn't such a bad place after all. . . . I shall never forget Mrs. Mac's kindness to me. She was really a mother during those days at school. . . . To me, as to all of us "Mrs. Mac" has and always will be, part of St. Andrew's, and probably the gentlest and most pleasant part. . . . I will always remember Mrs. Macdonald as very kindly and sympathetic during my years at St. Andrew's College especially to home-sick boys. . . . I don't think I shall ever forget how good Mrs. Macdonald was to all of us while she was at St. Andrew's—she was a real mother to us all. . . . I look back, however, on 1905 at St. Andrew's as one of the happiest and most care-free years of my life and realize that this was in no small measure due to the home-like atmosphere created by Mrs. Macdonald and yourself. . . . I shall always remember her very kindly and motherly interest in us all at old St. Andrew's. . . . I am continually reminded of the time when I was at the College. I was far from home and the kind interest of Mrs. Macdonald will always be remembered. . . . Her memory is very precious to me and I know to all the other boys who came under her spell. We are grateful for that contact. . . . I have a very great affection for her and I cannot recall those grand days at St. Andrew's without remembering the very important part she played in them, and what great interest and affection she always had in our activities. . . . It is rather wonderful to reflect upon the manner in which your wife during her lifetime, and from the moment she was married to you and came to St. Andrew's, completely entered into your own life-work in building up a National Institution. . . . Mrs. Macdonald was so kind to all of us as schoolboys, as well as a true friend after College days were over, that I am sure all Old Boys who were fortunate enough to be at St. Andrew's whilst she was there, will feel a great personal loss now that she has gone. . . . I will always remember her as one of the really beautiful people I have known. . . . We will never forget the loving and kindly way Mrs. Macdonald treated all the boys and was truly a mother to us. . . . Only one who has been at the School can appreciate Mrs. Macdonald's wonderful influence on every boy who had the privilege of knowing her. . . . And with her kindness went much wise advice. I know that many others have had the same experience. . . . Her courage was indomitable. I never knew of anyone with a greater store of sympathy for others. . . . All the time that I was at St. Andrew's College I'm sure that the rest of the boys and myself had no greater friend and supporter than Mrs. Macdonald."

They rest from their labours and their works follow them.

The man who would be truly happy should not study to enlarge his Estate, but to contract his Desires.—Plato.

A MAN should not, if he wish to be truly happy, try to enlarge his estate but be satisfied with what he has. As far as personal convenience and condition of his finances go, a man should do his best to make all the money he can, and should be satisfied that he is doing this. Otherwise he is letting himself and his family down. If a man is sure that he is doing this, however, he should not care how much or how little money he is making, but be satisfied with what he has and make the best of it. What happiness is there for a man who is never satisfied—in other words a man who is always disappointed? Disappointment certainly is not happiness.

Let us take a man like Napoleon for example. He was never really happy. He may have had power, but the more power he got the more he wanted. His life, as you know, ended in disaster.

Also, if you looked into the private lives of many of the millionaires of to-day, you would find that they spent a great deal of the time worrying—worrying about how to make more money or fearing that they were going to lose what they had. On the other hand, there are thousands of young people in this world who have not much of anything, and yet they get more enjoyment out of life than most people. Why? Because they are satisfied. Satisfaction is the gateway to happiness.

Part of the lyric of a negro folk-song by the late George Gershwin goes like this:

>I got plenty o' nuthin',
>And nothing's plenty fo' me;
>Oh! I got no car; got no mule;
>>got no misery.
>The folks with plenty o' plenty
>They got a lock on the do':
>Afraid somebody's a gonna rob 'em while
>They's out making mo'
>What fo'?

These words illustrate my point. If we boil it down to one sentence it is this: Do the best you can in life and be satisfied that you cannot have everything. Be thankful for having anything at all.

FLEMMING, Form V.

Looking east from about the centre of the College property.

A YOUNG man, swathed in a poor-fitting raincoat, hastily paid his taxi-fare and walked out into the teeming rain which was pouring relentlessly on the main thoroughfare of the city of Lesterville. He peered ahead intently through the dense screen of water until his eyes lit on another man standing in the shadow of the doorway of an apartment building, engaged in viciously biting off the end of a cigar. The young man hastened up to the stranger and tapped him gently on the shoulder. "John," he murmured in a voice vibrant with emotion.

The other looked up, after fiercely shoving a soaked and unlightable cigar back into the recesses of his overcoat pocket. "Were you addressing me?" he inquired harshly.

"Is it you?" cried the young man, huskily. "Are you my brother, John Graham?"

The only reply was the incessant beat of the rain on the pavement.

"I am Philip Graham," he continued. "I left my brother in a dreadful rage twenty years ago. But I've discovered that I was wrong. I put an advertisement in all the big papers of the country arranging a meeting here. It has cost me a fortune, but if you are he, it will be well worth it."

There was still no reply.

"Tell me, are you John?" cried Philip.

"No," said the stranger, viewing a neighbouring bank out of the corner of his eye. "I'm not your brother." Then he slouched away a short distance.

Philip stood waiting at the spot for another fifteen minutes, perspiration mingling with the drops of rain. Then he hailed a taxi, and rode away. A contemptuous laugh floated from the lips of the stranger out into the watery air. Then he looked at his watch and murmured, "Plenty of time." And then, fiercely, "I hope Jiggs remembers to bring the extra gun. This robbery ain't going to be easy." Then he started as a tall figure loomed up in front of him.

"Hello, Tony," murmured the newcomer. "I'm all ready for the job."

"You're too early, Jiggs," muttered the other, frowning slightly, "I didn't expect you this early. I have to be here to watch the bank in case anything happens which might spoil our plans. But you're away ahead of time. Why?"

"Oh, I just thought I'd come," was the hazy reply.

"Did you remember to bring the extra gun?" asked Tony.

Jiggs, shaking visibly, muttered, "No; I forgot." Then he looked from side to side, scrutinizing the gloom.

"Fool," cried Tony. "You didn't have to come this early. If you had waited, you might have remembered."

The silence which ensued was broken by a clap of thunder which echoed and re-echoed about the streets.

Tony wiped the moisture from his face. "Talking of fools," he said, "I just met a guy, who was here waiting for his long-lost brother whom he had advertised for in the paper. Sentimental sap!"

Jiggs staggered back as another clap of thunder pierced the monotonous beating of the rain. "Good God!" he cried, "my brother. I was too late after all."

WILSON, Form VI.

A Hundred Years Ago

THE Rebellion of 1837 was an unfortunate incident in the history of Upper Canada, but the investigation into its causes and the report presented to the British Government by Lord Durham mark the beginning of Responsible Government and the dawn of a new epoch in the history of the British Empire. Every incident of this petty affair has an interest even after the passing of a hundred years. In 1837 there stood on Yonge Street, on the grounds of St. Andrew's College, a building then known as McLeod's Tavern. After the battle of Montgomery's Tavern, in which the forces of Lount and Mackenzie were defeated, this tavern became a rallying point of the Loyalist forces.[1] A day or two after the battle there was a movement to burn Lount's house, which stood on upper Yonge Street. His wife secured the assistance of a neighbour's boy and

a yoke of oxen and sent her household goods down Yonge Street, presumably to her father-in-law's house, which still stands on the hill opposite the school. The boy, whose name was Stephen Howard, was arrested and spent some uncomfortable hours in the old tavern till his father, a respectable Quaker, secured his release. McLeod's Tavern was still standing in 1927 and was occupied for some time by our cricket coach, Harry Davis. Its original owner, Murdoch McLeod, had been a fierce opponent of the Family Compact.[2] The first settler on the St. Andrew's property (lot 84) was Philip Cody (of Huguenot descent), grandfather of Colonel Cody (Buffalo Bill). In 1806 Philip Cody sold his farm to Murdoch McLeod for a thousand dollars, and in 1823 Murdoch McLeod sold the south half to Daniel McLeod for two thousand. It is probable that Philip Cody's log house, built in 1799, stood on the same site as the tavern. There were plenty of wolves and bears and Indians in those days.

P. J. R.

[1] Lindsey, *Life and Times of W. Lyon Mackenzie*. [2] Scadding, *Toronto of Old*, p. 107.

If Only Fiction Were The Truth

"UNTIL we meet again, comrades." The sleek, silvery door swung to, noiselessly, as the well-tuned motors roared to life. With a cheery wave, Comrade Taschov hurtled his glistening bird into the dense fog. The comrade in charge of aviation followed the trail of the 'plane closely with his glasses, until invisible, and the hum of the motors was no longer audible. With an uneasy sigh, this worried individual entered his car, just as dawn was breaking over the aerodrome.

Days pass, gradually lengthening into weeks, but still no reply to the frantic tap, tap, tap of the operator's key, vainly trying to contact the six airmen. Search parties from four countries, headed by experienced airmen, disperse over the vast Arctic spaces, but their search is fruitless. They return, some dejected and despairing, others clinging to the hope that sometime, somewhere.....

.... "Comrade, ask for further weather bulletins." Voices are heard above the roar of the motors..... "Heavy fog, low visibility, increased wind velocity." ... The ship lurches, lunges, and plummets earthward. .... "To the tail, hurry!" But there is no need for the command, as already a huddled group has formed. A sickening thud, the screech of twisted metal, the stillness.

.... "Two loaves, one dozen chocolate bars, bandages," this in a meticulous tone, "we can last only a week longer. Our comrades," motioning to the two inert forms huddled in blankets on the floor of the cabin, "are in need of a doctor's care, or else ..." The voice stopped.

.... "Comrade, you and I alone have strength left in our bodies. I am setting out for an Eskimo village, which is charted approximately one hundred miles from this spot. If I make it," his voice broke, "I will return in a week. If I do not return ...", he handed his companion a loaded revolver, "it is for the best." With that, he emerged into the flurrying, eddying snowflakes, and quickly disappeared from view.

Then followed days of tortuous plodding through snow, intermittently plunging through thin ice, spending a night on an ice floe, the thought gradually dawning that hands and feet were becoming useless. Days filled with insane visions, wild dreams, as he dragged one foot past its mate.

He was picked up on the fifth day by some Eskimos, who were hunting seals, after they had shot at his limp bulk stretched on the ice, mistaking him for their prey. Sufficiently recovered, he rallied his remaining strength and hoarsely whispered the story.

Six sleds immediately set out, following his instructions and rough calculations. The dogs hauled at their traces nobly when the wrecked monster was sighted. Approaching nearer, a figure framed itself in the doorway, let out a choked sob, and collapsed in the arms of an Eskimo.

The trip back was accomplished with greater speed. Long hours of careful nursing by Eskimo mothers, and days of convalescence in the sun, soon returned the health of all six Russians. Father Dabriel, flying to the outpost in his mission 'plane, learnt the news and the outside world soon knew the glad tidings.

Two months later, the comrade in charge of aviation was once again eagerly watching a mammoth of the skies, this time in descent. Taxiing to a standstill, the pilot cut the motors, and simultaneously six figures leapt to the ground, to be embraced by wives and relatives. The comrade in charge of aviation pushed his way through the milling throng, and embraced Comrade Taschov. With tears in his eyes, he said, "We meet again, comrade."

THOMSON I, Form VI.

Stanley Comes Across

IT was one of those perfect fall afternoons—crisp and sunny, with leaves on the ground and a tang in the air. Stanley Hare, the hardworking father of a happy North York family of hares, was reclining in the sun after rather overeating at lunch. He was warm and comfortable and thoroughly at peace with the world, for he had promised himself that the next fine day that came along he would take the afternoon off and thoroughly enjoy himself doing nothing. And now that day had come in exactly the form for which he had hoped. Stanley heaved a long sigh of contentment and closed his eyes for an afternoon nap.

At that moment, however, Mrs. Hare, who had been sitting at the back door chatting with Gerald, the cat from the neighbouring farm, called over her shoulder, "Stanley dear, I'm sorry to disturb you, but Gerald here says that those pesky beagles are coming up again this afternoon, and I reallly do think that you should give them a bit of a run. The St. Andrew's boys are sure to be out with them, and you know how disappointed they would be."

"Oh bother," grunted Stanley, rolling over and opening one eye. "Why should I give up the one free afternoon I've had for weeks to amuse a mob of schoolboys. Besides its becoming rather a dangerous thing. Those hounds are terribly liable to get excited and carry the thing too far, especially as there are so many of them this year."

"Now Stanley, don't be a kill-joy. Just a circle of a mile or so ending at home again would do perfectly,—or even a straight run to cousin Mary's. The boys simply love those bits through the woods."

"Oh, all right then," Stanley replied, "just to please you, my dear."

And thus it was that that run of November 11th came to be. And if this should happen to get into the hands of Stanley Hare, I am sure that I shall be expressing the feelings of all the school by thanking him very much for a most enjoyable afternoon.

VI FORMER

The Naval Review

SHORTLY after the Coronation, there took place at Spithead the greatest naval review that the world has yet seen. Two hundred mighty ships, representing not only Britain's power on the seas, but the power of almost every nation in the world, were assembled at that time in honour of England's newly crowned monarch.

Only the crews of that multitude of ships know the hours of arduous work that were done in preparation for the "great day." Fresh paint was applied in many places, decks were, as usual, scrubbed snow-white, and every piece of metal that would take a polishing was made to shine like a mirror. In addition to this regular routine, thousands of feet of electric wire and thousands of lights had to be prepared and hung for the fleet illuminations. Search-light crews had practised for days their intricate display, to be given on the night of the Review.

On the day of the great Review, the greater part of Britain's fleets were drawn up in three ten mile lines, off the historic channel port Portsmouth, headed by the flagship Nelson of the Home Fleet. The foreign and visiting vessels formed the fourth and last line. Banners, flags and streamers of countless colours and designs hung from the masts and rigging of every ship from smallest torpedo boat to H.M.S. Hood, the largest battleship afloat.

At one p.m. the crews and their officers in dress uniform "manned the side at the salute" all along the lines. As the stately Royal yacht appeared in the hazy distance, coming out of Portsmouth harbour, there began a magnificent succession of deafening salutes, a salvo of ten salutes being fired by each ship As the Royal yacht, followed by a procession of beautiful yachts bearing official guests, came opposite each ship, its crew gave three hearty cheers. The King and his admirals stood in full view on the bridge, at the salute.

Signals passed constantly between the Nelson and various other flagships throughout the afternoon About the middle of the afternoon the massed planes of the Fleet Air Arm flew past in formation.

At ten p.m. began the concluding fleet illuminations. A signal from the Nelson caused a magical transformation, as each ship burst into light simultaneously. The ships sprang into brilliance, each one being completely outlined by tiny pin points of light, even to such details as guns, turrets and funnels. It was a thrilling sight. Following this came a magnificent search-light display, the crews of all ships operating their lights in perfect time and to a definite routine. This gave marvellous effects, the bright fingers of light probing the clouds and weaving intricate patterns in the sky.

The concluding spectacle was a burst of seven foot rockets from the foredeck of each ship. From some ships golden waterfalls and huge pinwheels poured a blaze of light on the scene.

It was a never-to-be-forgotten sight, and a fitting climax to so great a day.

KILPATRICK I, Lower VI.

All That Glitters Is Not Gold

THE thief stopped in his tracks, as he felt someone lay a hand on his hunched shoulder. He knew who it was before he turned around.

"Well, my little honest man, why are you walking past a jewelry store for the third time at two o'clock in the morning?"

"Now Jim, just because you're a cop now, it doesn't mean that you're going to break up our schoolboy friendship, does it?"

"If you have any brains, you'll be gone from here the next time I pass. I never thought you'd turn out to be a crook, but I think you can be cured, and I'll do it."

"No one will ever catch me," bragged Swifty Cordone, as he walked around the corner to the side entrance of the jewelry store. The policeman, Jim Macpherson, entered the store by his pass key, and made his way to the bag of valuable jewels.

As he was coming out he heard a loud yell for help and started down the street on the run. He carelessly left the door open behind him. Swifty, who had been standing around the corner, saw all this through the glass windows. He rounded the corner at full speed and entered the door without so much as a glance down the street. Reaching the counter, he picked up a large bag, which the jeweller always left on the counter so that the policeman would see it as he was passing. This bag was known to contain many valuable jewels and was the main objective of every thief in town. At least once a night the policeman entered the store and inspected the bag. This bag was said to be worth about twenty thousand dollars, and this system of guarding was subject to much ridicule in the town. Swifty took the bag and ran out the store door; he kept on running till he got home. He wisely decided to lie low for a couple of days until the fuss, which he thought would undoubtedly arise, blew over.

In the meantime Mr. Alexis Gornoff, the jeweller, had been called by Macpherson the morning after the robbery.

"Well sir," said Jim, "I guess it worked. The bag was gone when I got back."

"Insert the advertisement then, Jim. That was mighty fine work. I'll see that you get a bonus."

The next day, instead of blazing headlines as Swifty expected, there was a little paragraph in the advertising section entitled "All That Glitters Isn't Gold."

"This morning at two o'clock a burglar by the name of Cordone entered a jewelry store and took a supposedly valuable bag of jewels from Mr. Gornoff's counter. We imagine Mr. Cordone does not know that they were the best jewels Woolworth's had for a dollar and a quarter. Mr. Gornoff would be obliged to him if he returned said valuable jewels. Cordone will not be arrested, as he has been taught a good lesson."

Poor Swifty, who wasn't bad at heart and didn't like the idea of jail, grabbed the bag and ran all the way to Gornoff's. When he reached Gornoff's private office he noticed that Macpherson was there too.

"Well Swifty, have you been taught a lesson?" demanded Macpherson.

"I should say so," responded poor Swifty, giving the bag to Mr. Gornoff, "may I go now?"

"Yes, but you know what will happen to you if it occurs again."

Swifty knew only too well and left the room in a hurry, never to steal another thing in his life. After he had gone Gornoff proceeded to dump the fake bag into the waste-paper basket when a piece caught his eye.

"By the way Jim, which bag did you put on the counter?"

"Oh—the one on the first shelf. Why?"

"Oh! my God," screamed Gornoff. "Are we lucky? That was the bag of real jewels. Cordone had the real jewels all the time!"

"This was certainly more real than I thought it would be. Your wife, who was supposed to yell for help, was really in trouble because she had just been run over when I came to her. She didn't want me to tell you, but I had to!"

Mr. Gornoff fainted before the constable had finished speaking.

Sitting On The Back Bridge—November, 1937.

I think the God that planned these lakes and fields
And cities of our northern British land
Made Winter month on month and then the Spring,
Delaying Summer's advent such a time
That Summer does not recognize itself,
Until these Fall-Term autumn days and nights.
How else could there be crowded in these months
The very climax of our season's fare?
Morning and evening mists and coloured skies,
The cricket's final universal chirp,
Cool smells of stocks, and mint, and nicotine,
The clear, queer shunting of a distant train
—All reach St. Andrew's sense subconsciously
Until November's slow-approaching frost
Stills all of them. Yet as the players in
Some patient orchestra will mute their strings
Until the meet finalé is resolved,
So do Aurora's sights and sounds and smells
All bide their time until the directing sun
Says, "Up! November's come! One last slow bar!"
These are the days—the Indian's summer-time
When all the season's offerings gather up
The best they have, and giving, slowly go.
Does Nature thus arrange in other lands?
I like to think that only Canada
Can reap so sweet a harvest of the mind.

October Sky, 1937 (Camera Club,—Sheppard)

Précis of Dr. Kilpatrick's Sermon

SERMON—What is man?
TEXT—*"Run now through the streets and seek and see if ye can find me a a man". Jeremiah 5:1.*

IT was a small paragraph used to fill in an incompleted page in a magazine that suggested to me the line I want to follow to-night. This paragraph was headed, "What are you worth"? It was a simple chemical analysis of the human body and an estimate of its commercial value. From it I learn that a man is made up of the following:

Enough sulphur to put in the dog's drinking water.
Enough lime to whitewash a chicken coop.
Enough fat to make six bars of soap.
Enough iron to make a six penny nail.
Enough phosphorus for twenty boxes of matches.
Enough sugar for ten cups of tea.
Enough potassium to explode a toy cannon.

The remaining 75% of the body, H_2O, = plain water. Total value—87 cents.

I sat and stared at that for a time feeling rather small. That is a man reduced to chemical terms and with a price tag of 87 cents: Plato, Shakespeare, the Carpenter of Nazareth and kings and princes of the race could be so described. Take a human being into the laboratory and all that comes out is a handful of chemicals. Take the chemicals into the market and you'll get 87 cents for them and that completes the humiliation. And, mark you, that *is* a true description of a man, so far as it goes, but there is none here who feels the final word has been said about man when the chemist is done with him. Indeed something rises within us to protest this as a description of a man at all. An analysis of his body if you like, but not an account of his nature, not a definition of his being. "Know thyself", said the old Greek maxim, and it is vital, if we are to make any worthy use of life, that we should know the truth about ourselves. We simply can't accept the verdict that we're only worth 87 cents: there are aspects of our nature on levels where a cash value does not apply.

Now I don't propose to go into a discussion of human nature with you. But one thing is clear, you haven't given even a tolerable description of a man till you have taken account of the fact that he knows the difference between right and wrong; that is, he has a moral nature and he has a capacity and instinct for faith in spiritual realities, which is to say he is a religious being. And I hold that these two aspects of manhood, the moral side and the spiritual side, are not only as significant as his physical nature but far more so. The man who treats himself merely as an animal, gratifying his appetites and ignoring duty, honour, unselfishness, the moral qualities of his nature, that man dishonours himself. You certainly haven't said the vital thing about a man when you describe him as an animal governed by the urge to feed his body and reproduce his kind.

Look at two contrasting pictures. I don't need to draw the first; you have seen a drunkard, a sensualist, a glutton. It's an ugly picture, but that is a man, though you'll all admit it is not a man at his best. Why do we instinctively feel that in that condition a man has sunk in the scale? Isn't it precisely because we all think of manhood in terms of finer things? Take this picture: "A young student of theology named Maclean had gone out one morning from his home in the little fisher town on the Moray Firth to do forenoon's reading in a quiet spot by the sea, when he saw a boy, a stranger in the place, going out into the waters that he knew were dangerous. He cried out to him to warn him, but the boy took no heed. After a while Maclean heard a cry out at sea, and looking up he saw that the boy was struggling with the current. He laid his books down, and made straight for the water with a plank he had somehow got hold of on the way. He got up to the lad in time, and as the current swept them both outward, tried in vain to get him on the plank. But the lad was exhausted, and again and again slipped off. Then he felt his own strength giving out, but persisted and at last succeeded, and saved his man. But his own powers were exhausted and he sank and was drowned." McLean didn't sit down and reason out his action: he responded to something in himself which set his feet to the sea and to the rescue. That's a man! Which picture will you take as your conception of manhood? There's no need to ask this company. MacLean and his kind represent man at his best. We have moved a long way from the merely animal. Something has brought us from the night of the vanished ages, up from the primeval slime to a being endowed with courage and unselfishness, infinitely removed in the secapacities from the level of a creature with merely physical appetites.

Every man has to take his choice between these two conceptions of manhood. And to choose the higher is to face the price demanded of him who would be a man. For, mark you, there is nothing surer than this, that you'll have a fight on your hands between the lower and the higher impulses of your being. I would not dishonour this company by questionining how they would vote in this issue. I want rather to hold up to you some of the qualities for which you have to strive if you would make proof of your manhood.

When I was away with one of the ships of the Navy, one day the admiral, Sir Matthew Best, talking to me about the Service, said this:

"The men of the Apollo, as of the whole British navy, are essentially gentlemen." That was a sincere tribute from one who knows the Navy better than most. Your Principal would say the same of the boys of St. Andrew's College; they are essentially gentlemen. Well, then, what are the marks of a gentleman? To what have you to live up, if you would justify your Principal's estimate of you? Out of all the qualities of a gentleman, I'm only going to mention two.

First, I would say that honour is a mark of a gentleman. He keeps his word; he scorns a lie; he is to be trusted. The discipline of any school to-day is a vastly different thing from what it was 100 years ago. Then it was maintained by methods which gave a large place to "brute force". To-day discipline, while it has and must have its outward restraints, is chiefly something you maintain yourselves because you are trusted. The name of the school is in your keeping. That, of course, means that the boy who will respond to that, as a gentleman, is not free to do what he likes. Wherever he goes the school crest proclaims him. He is not simply a private individual, he belongs to St. Andrew's College and if the sense of honour is alive in him he bears himself accordingly. The secret of high morale, of work well done, of pride in your belonging to the school, is in large measure this quality of honour, difficult to define, yet always recognizable as the mark of a gentleman. It has its own compelling power in a man's life. Quoting the Ten Commandments to a man might leave him cold; even the inflexible rules of the School may not be final for him, but touch him on the point of his honour and, unless he has fallen out of the ranks of manhood altogether, you have made out your case.

Secondly, chivalry is the mark of a gentleman. It is a high sounding word but it is easily translated into things we recognize and honour. It means the thing in a man which instinctively rises up to protect the weak, the defenceless, anybody in trouble. You know what you would do if you saw a bully knocking a small boy about or insulting a woman. It was that same instict which lay behind the solid public opinion of what Britain ought to do when Belgium was invaded in 1914. It is not a quality that must always have some dramatic situation to call it out. Life in this school is full of opportunity to display it for in common guise it means having a mind and heart for the other fellow and the whole spirit of this school turns on how far this quality is part of your lives. There was nothing more splendidly revealed in the War than this very thing. It is, thank God, the heritage of the common man of our race. During the battle of the Somme, a group of wounded men were lying in a sunken road waiting to be taken out by the ambulance. It was a hot day. They were all suffering desperately from thirst but the water supply was done. A padre happened along and the medical officer eagerly asked if he had any water. "Yes," he said, "I have my water-bottle. Taking this the doctor said, "Just a sip, boys, or there won't be enough to go round." From stretcher to stretcher the bottle passed and when the padre received it again it was *still full*. Every man had denied himself that the other fellow might have his share. Call it decency, or fair play, anything you like, that is chivalry and it's the mark of a gentleman.

There is only one other thing I must say. Chesterton once said, "If you want to make a thing living, make it local." There is little use in talking in vague general terms about great things; bring them down to earth. So it is with these ideals of manhood. Word pictures are little use. Show us these qualities in a life, then we'll have some hope that they are within reach. Surely God understood that feeling in a man's heart for He gave us Jesus Christ, the one perfect gentleman of the ages, to live out in human life the best we can ever know. I want you to know that Jesus of Nazareth was no plaster saint. He was a man among men. But, because of what He was, some of us feel that He was so far above our level of character that, whatever the word of God means to us, it is going to be all that Jesus Christ was and is. It may be a long time before I can speak to you again. If that be so, let my last word be of the living Christ who is in this school, eager to take these lives and fashion them after the strength of His own. Eager, yes—and able. There is not a boy of this company He cannot, if given the chance, change and strengthen and lift to new heights of character. "If given the chance", at the last you have to say whether you want to be made like Him. He believes that because of your need, yes, and because of the good in you, you will give Him your lives.

Boys of St. Andrew's, I salute you. I wish for you the best of all things that may befall,—that you will take your places in life, servants and followers, lovers of the Lord Jesus Christ.

Prize Day

THE presentation of prizes for the year 1936-37, was held on the fifteenth of June, too late to be reported in our last number.

Many parents and friends of the boys took advantage of the fine weather to attend. As has been the custom in the past, the proceedings were held in the gymnasium, which was attractively arranged for the occasion. It was a very fitting finale to those who were to go out from the school into the world. It was an inspiration to those who were leaving for the holidays only.

The ceremonies were begun by a prayer and a reading from the psalms, by the Rev. G. O. Lighbourn. After the Headmaster had delivered his address, Mrs. J. H. Chipman, on behalf of the 48th Highlanders Chapter of the I.O.D.E. presented the rifle for shooting competition to Shields I. Sir Joseph Flavelle, after a short speech, presented the prizes to the Lower School boys. Dr. Bruce Macdonald then said a few words and presented the remaining shooting prizes. The guest speaker, Dr. G. D. Kilpatrick delivered a most interesting and inspiring speech, which few of us will ever forget. Dr. Kilpatrick then presented the remaining prizes, and the National Anthem was sung. Tea was served to the visitors in the quadrangle.

The prize winners were as follows:

J.F.M.

GENERAL PROFICIENCY PRIZES

Form IA.—1st, Rapmund, G. L.
Form IB.—1st, Beverly, W. A.
Form II.—1st, Langley, A. E. J.; Special, O'Hara I, J. W.
Form III.—1st, Graham, R. L.; 2nd, Cobban, W. A.; 3rd, Hunter, D. C.; 4th, Williams I, J. R. M.
Form IV.—1st, Mitchell II, D. M.; 2nd, Hampton II, L. G.; 3rd, Grass II, R.; Special, Flemming, D. P.
Form V.—1st, Wilson, M. T.; 2nd, Senior, C. R. A.; 3rd, MacIntosh I, D. G. K.; Special Prize, Kilpatrick I, D. B.

General Course.—1st, King, W. D.
Lower VI.—1st, Cockfield, A. S.; 2nd, Bonnell, E. D.; 3rd, Kent, M. G.; Special, O'Brian, J. A.
Upper VI.—1st, Gerhart, T. L.; 2nd, Kilgour, A. R.; 3rd, Eakins, J. W.
Writing and Spelling.—MacLaren, K. F.
Scripture Prize.—Mitchell II, D. M.
Wyld Prize in Latin. (Mrs. W. B. McPherson & Mrs. Sifton.)—Spence II, [D. B.
Isabelle Cockshutt Prizes in History. (Mrs. Henry Cockshutt.)—Thompson I, A. S.; Connacher, H. B. F.
Hulbig Medal in Mathematics. (Mr. Sidney Hulbig.)—Archibald, H. E.
Old Boys' Medal in Mathematics.—Gerhart, T. L.
Ashton Medal in English. (Mr. Charles Ashton.)—Spence II, D. B.
Cooper Medal in Science.—Gerhart, T. L.
Georges Étienne Cartier Medal in French. (Mr. Jack Beer)—Gerhart, T. L.
Chairman's Gold Medal.—Bonnell, E. D.
Lieut. Governor's Silver Medal.—Gerhart, T. L.
Lieut. Governor's Bronze Medal.—Cockfield, A. S.
Headmaster's Medal.—Gerhart, T. L.
Governor General's Medal.—Gerhart, T. L.
Macdonald Medal.—Dickie, D. M.
48th Highlander's Chapter of the I.O.D.E. (Rifle)—Shields I, C. M.
Christie Cup. (Mrs. R. J. Christie)—Seaton, J. D.
Gordom Thorley Medal.—MacIntosh I, D. G. K.
Lawrence Crowe Medal.—McCoubrey, A. F.
Cricket Cup.—Pentland, W. T.

THE BEAGLE HUNT

On Thursday, November 11th, Mr. Snowden's Beagles started a run from the school. We all enjoyed it—we were all invited— and look forward to another hunt next fall. They got a hare.

MR. FINLAY'S WORLD CRUISE

Mr. Finlay is always sure of a warm welcome. He was kind enough to tell us about a voyage he made in a coast-guard vessel out of Hong Kong last summer, and was extremely interesting. Time ran against us all, for before he had got us back safely in port, the bell rang for prayers. We really want to hear the finale to his experience and hope that the winter term's "Lits" will afford us, and him, a suitable opportunity.

M.T.W.

CAMERA CLUB

Again under the genial aegis of Mr. J. Y. S. Ross the Camera Club is active. Meetings have been held regularly, and so many photographs have been submitted for publication in this number that the editors have found it difficult to select those they did.

Mr. Ross has built a remarkably good developing mechanism—a large revolving cylinder in a tray—for the modern long films. The enlarging machine is busier than ever. Heintzman turned up with a small Leica F. 2 which has produced some great speed pictures. We are looking forward to the annual exhibition in the spring, and to obtaining some good pictures for the Summer number of the Review.

J.C.

Locate this spot. (Camera Club,—Sheppard)

PING PONG

It is with some trepidation that I submit this. The athletic director told the staff adviser that he hoped it wouldn't go with the sporting news, and I don't know whether ping-pong is a sport or not. The dictionary says for *"sport," "fun or diversion," "a pastime of an outdoor or athletic kind."* We play it indoors, and it is certainly fun and or diversion. At any rate we have this year revivified the old in-between-season ping-pong tables in the basements of both houses, and have snaffled balls and bats from all possible quarters. Flavelle House got a little cocky about their ping-pong, so we took them on and trimmed them hands down by a score of 3-2 out of five matches. We won't admit that it was close,—which it was. Memorial House was obviously superior.

Progressive ping-pong is hot-stuff between dinner and study, or prayers and first warning. We are indebted to Mr. Smith for the help he has given to ping-pong.

M.T.W.

THE FOOTBALL DINNER

Mr. Joe Breen and Mr. Bobby Porter were the guests of the school at the Football Dinner on November 22nd.

The First Team, the Captains of the Seconds, Thirds, and Fourths, and the six masters who had coached teams met the Headmaster in the decorated Upper School dining-room. Elaborate preparations had been made: shaded lights hung over the big T-shaped table, in the centre of which were dozens of football players rampant on a field vert.

Mr. Breen, in an inspiring speech, proposed a toast to the School. Nobody could ever have been listened to more attentively; from his wealth of football experience he told us what he thought really mattered in playing football, and the part played by the individual and the team. Mr. Ketchum briefly replied, stating his views on the importance of football and its incorporation into the whole school life. To the toast to the School, Captain Seaton replied in excellent sense and taste; he then presented the Coach, Bobby Porter, with two engraved steins. Amid loud applause, Mr. Porter managed to be heard. One thing your reporter remembers particularly was that our coach, who had played on Dominion Senior Champion teams (as had Mr. Breen too) in all his games of football, hockey, and professional baseball remembers with the most satisfaction one game,—and his team lost. It was when he was playing high school hockey and expected to be badly beaten by a team that was really good. His team, however, held them to a 2-1 score, and were very proud.

An unusually good conjuror and accordeon player rounded out the evening. Congratulations were forthcoming to Miss Robertson and her staff for the elegant dinner. It was a great evening. If talking football has anything to do with real playing,—we're great.

J.S.

Clouds from the Head's roof (Camera Club)

THE REVIEW congratulates one of our Board of Governors, Dr. G. G. D. Kilpatrick, M.A., who has been appointed to the Principalship of the United Theological College, affiliated with McGill University. We hope that his new responsibilities will not prevent us from seeing him as often as we have in the past.

The Chapel with some 1937 Clouds.—J.Y.S.R.

Chapel Notes

During October, when for purposes of health we confined ourselves to our own grounds, our usual practice of attending our respective churches in Aurora on Sunday morning was temporarily discontinued; instead, short morning services were held in the Chapel, and these we enjoyed. At the beginning of November we were again able to go to our Aurora churches.

On the first Sunday evening of Term, the Headmaster spoke to us and reminded us that in our struggle to attain perfect manhood there must be a threefold and harmonious development of mind, body and spirit. At subsequent services, interesting addresses were given by Dr. Robinson, Mr. Fleming, Mr. Tudball and Mr. O'Brian.

Professor George Glazebrook has often spoken to us in the past and he was good enough to address us again on October 24th. On November

14th, Dr. Kilpatrick preached one of his characteristic sermons the substance of which is reported elsewhere in this number.

Professor E. A. Dale visited us for the first time on November 28th and spoke to us in Chapel. On the following Sunday, the Rev. Gerald Burch preached to us; he is an Old Boy of the School and we always look forward to his sermon. On December 12th we are to be addressed by the Rev. A. P. Brace of the National Council of the Y.M.C.A.

We are more than grateful to all these genelemen who have so willingly given us of their time and who have so greatly helped to lend inspiration to the Sunday evening services.

A short memorial service was held in the Chapel at 11 a.m. on Armistice Day. Dr. Robinson read the roll of Andreans who gave their lives in the Great War—a roll which seems to grow longer with the years.

The funeral service for Mrs. Macdonald was held in the Chapel—her Chapel—on the afternoon of October 23rd. Many of the boys attended together with a throng of Old Boys, Governors and old friends of Mrs. Macdonald. Dr. Cody conducted the service which was impressive and beautiful.

On the last Sunday morning of Term, the usual communion service will be conducted by the Rev. G. O. Lightbourn.

For the greater part of this Term, the Lesson at the week-day morning services has been read in turn by members of the Upper and Lower Sixth Forms. The reading on the whole has been good, but there is still room for improvement in enunciation.

We have been busily practising for the annual Carol Service which is to be held on the last Sunday evening of Term. Although we are drawing freely on Carols sung in former years, a few new ones are being added and the service promises to be as beautiful as ever. As in the past, most of the singing will be in unison, but variety is added by special parts and verses for cantors and trebles.

M.T.W.

Au College

Déjà comme un foyer tout m'attire,
Tout me semble beau, grand, et spacieux,
Et moi qui pensait endurer le martyr
Déjà je me vois si heureux.

Devant nos yeux s'étend un vaste paysage,
La nature de ses beautés nous fait l'offrande;
De partout elle porte sur notre passage
Et les chansons de l'oiseau que tous aiment entendre.

Combien de choses magnifiques déjà
J'effleurai sans le savoir,
Mais comment pourrais-je aimer les lilas
Sans déjà les avoir?

Et dans un épais feuillage nous marchons
A travers un décor plein de gaieté et de joie,
Dans la paix et l'inconnu où nous allons
Oue de notre couvent nous trouvons dans tous les bois.

Et dans ces sentiers monotones
Combien de collines, combien d'obstacles,
Où déjà disparaît l'automne,
Et les fleurs de ce bois, quel spectacle!

J.M.L.

RUGBY

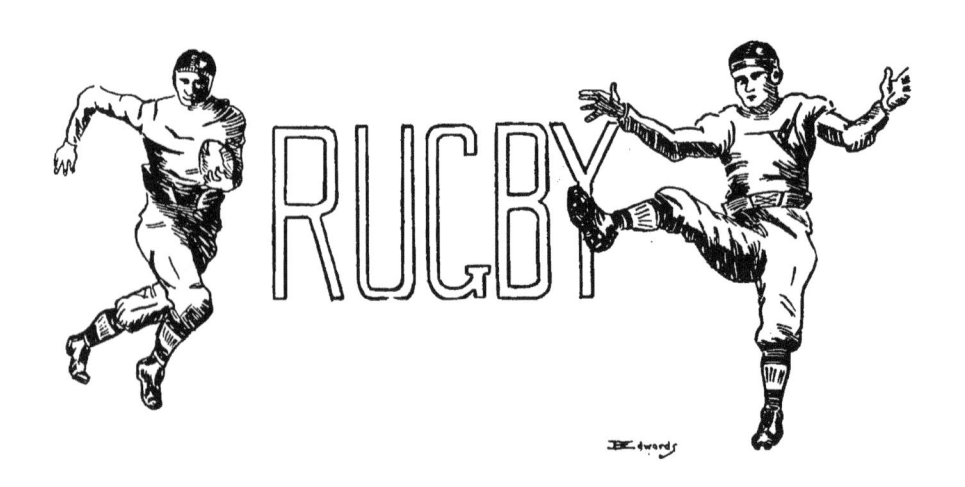

FIRST TEAM FOOTBALL

As there was but one old colour back, and the season was very late in starting, hopes for this year's success were not rosy. Under the able coaching of Mr. Bobby Porter, however, a good team was built up with some of last year's first and second squads and a few new boys. Hard conditioning began at once, and all ranks were very keen.

The only victory to record is one over Lakefield whom we defeated 33-0. In all other games, with the possible exception of the very first one, a good brand of football was displayed, and no score was overwhelming. In the Little Big Four games, we appeared at our worst, with due respect to our able opponents, against T.C.S., to whom we fumbled away a two point margin. The line proved to be the best we have had for three or four years, and the backs got steadily better as the season progressed. With a good kicker in the school, an entirely different story might be told. It is not wise to look too far ahead, but if this year's enthusiasm all through the football of the school may be reckoned with, and if we get as good coaching again, we ought to have a satisfactory season next year.

Seaton was elected Captain early in the season and was at all times an inspiration to his team.

Colours were awarded as follows: Seaton I, Allespach I, Bonnell, Christie, Hollinger II, Kent, Kinley, Macdonald I, MacIntosh I, Macrae, Mitchell I, O'Brian I, Rogers.

FIRST RUGBY TEAM

First Row—Left to Right: K. E. Rogers, G. C. Kinley, G. J. Christie, J. D. Seaton, D. G. Macrae, J. H. Mitchell, J. F. Macdonald.

Second Row—Left to Right: W. T. Hollinger, E. D. Bonnell, T. C. Gordon, W. D. Reid, D. G. K. MacIntosh, B. W. Allespach.

Third Row—Left to Right: R. A. Porter Esq. (Coach), W. D. Knight, J. A. O'Brian, Kenneth Ketchum Esq, M. G. Kent, Rutiff Grass, J. F. Macdonald.

The Appleby Game

Very soon after the opening of school, the first team played Appleby at Oakville, October 20th. There was a dry field with a moderate wind from the north-west.

After five minutes' play St. Andrew's scored a touch, Christie carrying the ball over and MacIntosh failing to convert. Before the first quarter was over, Alley plunged through for a touchdown for Appleby, tying the score. The tackling of Seaton and Christie stood out in this quarter.

S.A.C. seemed a little disconcerted by the blowing of a whistle instead of a horn, for off-sides. Appleby scored two touchdowns in the second quarter, both converted; Gudgeon scored the first, and Marlatt the second after a fumbled catch near our line. Before half time, McBride, for Appleby, kicked with the wind to the deadline. Half time score: Appleby 18, S.A.C. 5.

The third quarter was played with no scoring; we carried the ball to their territory only to lose it on fumbles. St. Andrew's forced the play in the last quarter, Macrae and Mitchell combining nicely on several occasions, and many forward passes being tried. No scoring was made, however, and the game ended 18-5 for Appleby. Congratulations to them.

S.A.C.: Seaton, Macrae, Mitchell, Rogers, Bonnell, Gordon, O'Brian, Hollinger, Allespach, Kent, Archibald, Macdonald, MacIntosh, Kinley, Knight, Davison, Grass, Angus, McCormick, Ankenmann.

Appleby: Beardmore, Magee, Alley, Baylay, Gudgeon, Leitch, Milsap, Ross, Williams, McBride, Marlatt, Robertson, Rising, Gzowski, Reid, Walker, Wigle.

The Lakefield Game

Playing the second game of the football season the first team engaged Lakefield on the latter's field on October 27th. Here we won our first victory of the schedule by overpowering a decidedly lighter team.

S.A.C. elected to kick off, the ball going fairly deep in Lakefield territory. The ball changed hands several times before any score was made. In the latter part of the first quarter MacIntosh kicked a placement, giving the reds a three point lead, which was retained until the end of the quarter.

Soon after play resumed Rogers plunged for 5 more points. His touch was converted by MacIntosh. Again with the ball in their territory we made another touchdown. This time Mitchell ran about 30 yards on a fast-breaking end run. St. Andrew's failed to convert. Their lost point, however, was made up for when Macrae tackled Rose behind the line. S.A.C. gained another touchdown on a long forward pass from Macdonald to MacIntosh, who, incidentally converted. Half-time was called with S.A.C. having 21 points, Lakefield none.

S.A.C. once more gained points at the beginning of the quarter when Seaton tackled Morley who fumbled. O'Brian recovered on the one yard line for S.A.C. Hollinger plunged over for another touch, which went unconverted. On a third down with ten yards to go, a pass was completed by Seaton. This gave us a first down. Being near the opponents' line MacIntosh kicked a rouge, and the period ended with the red team 27 points ahead.

In the last quarter S.A.C. again piled up points with another touchdown, an end run being the successful play. Rogers was the ball carrier. Macrae converted it. This ended the scoring for the game. The Lakefield team failed to cross the red's line once, the final score being 33-0 for S.A.C. Offensively our back field worked well, and by their passing, continually gained many yards. The line was the mainstay defensively. Only once did it seem likely that Lakefield would score; they were unable to do so, because of the strength and excellent blocking of our line.

S.A.C.—Seaton (captain), O'Brian, Hollinger II, Allespach I, Knight, Kent, Christie, Macrae, Macdonald I, Mitchell I, MacIntosh, Rogers. *Alternates*—Bonnell, Gordon, Grass, Kinley, Davison, Senior, Wadds, Ankenmann, Archibald, Reid, Angus.

Lakefield—Simpson, Morley, Rose, McLean, MacLaren, Pease I, Pease II, Foster, Crickmore, Frewer. *Alternates*—McGinnis, Carson, Roberts.

Upper Canada Game

The first Little Big Four game was played in Toronto on October 30th against U.C.C.

Seaton and Company. (Gardon)

We won the toss and took advantage in the first quarter of the strong wind that was blowing. Both teams played hard, fast football from the kick-off. St. Andrew's apparent hope of kicking down the field to a scoring position faded, when it was seen that, even with the wind, we gained nothing on an exchange of kicks with U.C.C.'s powerful punter, Corbett. S.A.C. gained on plunges and end runs, Mitchell and Allespach carrying well through the line. Upper Canada gained on end runs which began further out than our secondary expected; they seldom gained through the middle, owing to the great defensive work of our line and secondary defence there. Upper Canada scored a rouge, the only score in the first quarter.

1937 U.C.C. Game.

In the second quarter we appeared to make yards more often than they did; forwards were successfully completed off end runs to Seaton, and the line was standing up better than U.C.C.'s. Anything we gained, however, was discounted by the long Upper Canada kicks; MacIntosh and Macrae, with the sun in their eyes, caught these faultlessly and saved a score more than once. One more point was tallied, and the half time score was U.C.C. 2, S.A.C. 0

If St. Andrew's were going to win, the third quarter was the one to exploit. Macdonald scooped up a bouncing ball from the kick-off, and ran it back fifteen yards. Our plays came out with good timing; the U.C.C. end runs were no longer making gains. After ten minutes we scored a rouge, making the score 2-1. Our line broke through and blocked an Upper Canada kick, Mitchell falling on the ball and giving us possession on U.C.C.'s 3 yard line just as the three quarter whistle blew.

St. Andrew's chance to forge ahead came and went when Upper Canada held out two attempts of ours to buck the ball over. U.C.C. kicked out of danger, obtained possession about mid-field in due course, and then executed the big-scoring play of the day: a spectacular 40 yard forward was completed to Weir who eluded one S.A.C. back, and raced along the north side of the field for a touchdown which was converted. Score 8-1. St. Andrew's tried desperately to catch up in the last few minutes, often making good gains on forwards. Always, however, could U.C.C. put us back where we were by punting. The game ended with the ball on their 35 yard line.

For Upper Canada, Grant, and particularly Weir, appeared very fast indeed. Corbett kicked well. Their whole team appeared experienced and effective, although they looked a little tired at times.

Everyone on the S.A.C. team played well. The line worked like Trojans, the secondary was most effective, and the backs caught well. As in every other game this year, we suffered for the lack of a good kicker.

S.A.C.—Halves, Macdonald, MacIntosh, Rogers; flying wing, Bonnell; quarter, Macrae; snap, O,Brian; insides, Hollinger II, Allespach I; middles, Kent, Knight; outsides, Christie, Seaton (captain); subs, Kinley, Grass, Reid, Gordon.

U.C.C.—Halves, Weir, Grant, Lea; flying wing, Godefroy; quarter, Henderson; insides, K. D. Turnbull, Corbett; middles, Hastings, Simpson; outsides, Bongard, N. J. Turnbull; subs, Dearness, McCarthy, McKechnie, Anspach, Hart, Roberts, Heintzman, Bedell.

The T.C.S. Game

On Saturday, November 6th, the second Little Big Four game was played at Aurora against T.C.S. Quite a number of people came up to see the game, and fortunately it was a perfect rugby day.

From the kick-off the game was a hard one. The first score came early in the first quarter when Seaton fell on a T.C.S. fumble behind their line. There was no convert. Trinity, however, were not slow in replying, and Irwin broke away for a touchdown which he converted. The first quarter soon ended with the play still even.

In the second quarter, with the score standing at 6-5 for them, T.C.S. began to work some very effective four-man end runs. However, none of these got far enough to cause any scoring, and when finally Mitchell broke away on a long run to put the Saints in a scoring position, Macrae was able to carry the ball over for another touch which was converted by MacIntosh. This left the score at half-time at 11-6 for Saint Andrew's.

In the third quarter T.C.S.'s superior kicking began to tell, and they gradually bottled the Saints back in their own area. Several times Macrae ran out long Trinity punts to save the single points but finally the score came, and in a drastic way, for a T.C.S. man snaffled a fumble by Macrae and chalked up a touchdown which they failed to convert. Two more points kicked by Irwin completed the scoring.

The last quarter saw much open play and forward passing by the Saints as they tried vainly to overcome that two point lead. Mitchell ran well, and the line did heroic work, but all to no avail, and the final whistle blew with score still 13 to 11 for T.C.S.

For T.C.S. Beatty and Mood, outsides, tackled well and Irwin kicked very well. For Saint Andrew's the line was good, especially Seaton, the newly elected captain. Mitchell and Macrae starred in the back field.

T.C.S.—Half backs, Renison, McCullough, Hayes; quarter, Curtis; snap, Seagram; insides, Flemming, Russel; middles, Peacock, Wallace; outsides, Beatty, Mood. *Subs*—Marstone, Harvey, Partridge, Taylor.

S.A.C.—Half backs, Mitchell, Rogers, MacIntosh; quarter, Macrea; snap, O'Brian; insides, Hollinger, Allespach; middles, Kent, Kinley; outsides, Seaton, Christie. *Subs*—Gordon, Knight, Reid, Bonnell, Grass.

1937 Ridley Game. (Heintzman)

THE RIDLEY GAME

Wednesday, November 10th was a fine day for this important concluding game. It was a fast, clean game resulting in a victory for Ridley who gained 16 points to the Saint's 2.

S.A.C. kicked off, and shortly afterwards charged through a Ridley kick formation to obtain possession well in Ridley's territory, although we did not score; Ridley punted the ball well out. A long end run by Macrae followed by one with Bonnell on the end put the college back in Ridley ground. An attempted placement by S.A.C. failed, Ridley barely getting out with the ball. When Hodder tried to kick the ball out of danger, he was caught behind his own goal line for a safety touch. S.A.C. 2, Ridley 0. The play then shifted to S.A.C. territory, a cut-back putting Ridley on our one yard line. From there Gibbons carried the ball over for the first major score, on a trick reverse play. Hodder converted with a placement. Ridley soon secured a rouge. Later, a fumble gave Ridley the ball on the Saint's eighteen yard line. A beautifully screened fake placement gave Ridley their second touchdown. Ashburner swept wide around our left end. They failed to convert. Quarter time score 12-2 for Ridley.

In the second quarter Ridley worked the ball into position for a drop kick. Ashburner made the attempt, but it went wide for a single. The game remained fairly even from then till half time. Score 13-2 for the visitors.

In the third quarter Hodder for Ridley displayed some good kicking into the wind, and two rouges for them were secured.

The last quarter was closely fought. Ridley gained 22 yards on a statue of liberty play, Hodder to Ashburner, and from that position Hodder kicked another single. St. Andrew's rallied with a forward passing attack, and carried the ball to Ridley's ten yard line when the final whistle blew. Score: Ridley 16, St. Andrew's 2.

Ridley—Flying wing, Davidson; snap, MacDougall; halves, Hodder, Ashburner, Davison; quarter, Scandrett; outsides, Schmon, MacClelland; middles, Doherty, Lewis; insides, Gibbons, Langley; spares, MacIntosh, Tidy, Denison, Lopez, Edmonds, Newman.

St. Andrew's—Flying wing, Macdonald; halves, Mitchell, Reid, Bonnell; snap, O'Brian; quarter, Macrae; outsides, Seaton, Christie; middles, Kent, Kinley; insides, Allespach I, Hollinger II; spare, Gordon.

SECOND TEAM FOOTBALL

Much credit is due to that part of the First Squad of twenty-five boys in all, who did not make the First Team. The "scrubs" practised daily with the senior team. For the past couple of years they have had a short schedule of games against other schools. This probably interferred with the First Team practices, but it did seem to effect the greatest good for the greatest number. The difficulty was to select a second team in the middle of the season, for players would improve and sometimes play later in a First Team game.

The Seconds played two games against Pickering Juniors and one against Lakefield Firsts, not losing a game.

The following were awarded Second Colours: Angus, Ankenmann, Archibald, Davison, Gordon, Grass, Knight, McCormick, Reid.

S.A.C. Seconds vs. Pickering Seconds at Aurora

On Nov. 2nd, on home ground, S.A.C. Seconds tied Pickering Seconds with a score of 11 all.

48   *St. Andrew's College Review*

The running of Ankenmann and Bonnell for us, and that of Creed for Pickering featured a hard-fought and excellent rugby game.

The first quarter ended with both teams scoreless, after battling evenly at mid-field.

In the second quarter Pickering opened the scoring, when Lanier intercepted a wild forward pass from Archibald, and ran 60 yards for a touchdown, which was converted by a forward pass from Creed to Williams.

In the second half, however, the Saints rallied, and after some fine running by Bonnell, the ball was brought to Pickering's one-yard line. Davison secured a touchdown on a plunge, but Reid failed to convert.

SECOND RUGBY TEAM
First Row—Left to Right—H. H. Davison, G. J. Kinley, W. N. McCormick, E. D. Bonnell, W. D. Reid, H. E. Archibald, Ruliff Grass.
Second Row—Left to Right—R. R. Porter Esq. (Coach), W. D. Knight, R. D. Ankenmann, C. R. A. Senior, T. C. Gordon, W. G. Angus, J. A. Farrer.

Ankenmann then did some spectacular plunging and running, and once broke away for a thirty-five yard gain, only to be brought down within a few yards of the goal-line. A forward pass from Reid to Gordon resulted in another major score, which was not converted.

In the last quarter Pickering blocked a kick, and fell on the loose ball behind our line for a touchdown.

The last point was scored with a beautiful long kick by Reid, which went out of touch.

Final score: S.A.C. 11, Pickering 11.

S.A.C. Second Team vs. Lakefield Firsts

On the afternoon of Nov. 4th the Lakefield First Team played S.A.C. Second Team at Aurora, resulting in a win for the School of 11-0.

S.A.C. kicked off and held Lakefield to their own end of the field. Then a fumble gave Lakefield the ball which they kicked to the School's 25-yard line.

Early in the second quarter Gordon of S.A.C. went around the end for a good gain into Lakefield territory. Then Reid kicked for a point. The ball remained for some time near centrefield until Lakefield fumbled on receiving a kick to give S.A.C. the ball on their 15-yard line. This the School managed to push over for a touchdown by Davison, which was unconverted. The score at half time was 6-0 for S.A.C.

Lakefield kicked off to commence the second half but the ball was run back to centre field by Gordon. Even play followed until a 30-yard forward pass by Lakefield almost put them in a scoring position.

In the last quarter play began in School territory. A blocked kick gave S.A.C. the ball. Near the end of the game Ankenmann of S.A.C. broke away for a 50 yard run to the Lakefield 10 yard line. A short pass from Reid to Gordon resulted in a touchdown which was unconverted. The game ended with a score of 11-0 for S.A.C.

S.A.C. Seconds vs. Lakefield Firsts. Line-ups:

S.A.C. Second Team—Outsides, Sisman, Senior; middles, Knight, Davison; insides, Angus, Grass; snap, Wadds; quarter, McCormick; halves, Bonnell, Archibald, Reid, Ankenmann; flying wing, Gordon. Subs, Hampson, Broome.

Second Team return game at Pickering

The Seconds played again against Pickering Juniors on November 8th, this time at Newmarket.

The scoring started early in the first quarter when Pickering were smothered behind their line and we scored a rouge. The Seconds were carrying the play, and soon scored a touchdown, Hamilton carrying the ball at the end of a fast run. Knight converted. Score: S.A.C. 7, Pickering 0.

Pickering pressed hard in the second quarter, held us scoreless, and got into position for a field goal. Phipps, for them, put a placement between the uprights. Half time score 7-3.

The play was even in the third quarter. Pickering began throwing many forward passes, which seldom clicked, for the ball was wet. They scored a rouge when Hamilton, after catching a Pickering punt, was downed behind our line. The play see-sawed in the rain, until after a kick by Angus, Pickering fumbled behind their goal posts and Sisman fell on the ball for a St. Andrew's touch.

There was no score in the fourth quarter. Final score S.A.C. 12, Pickering 4. For St. Andrew's, everybody played well, Broome, Gordon and McCormick perhaps deserving special mention. For Pickering, Phipps starred.

S.A.C.—Grass, Wadds, Angus, Knight, Davison, Senior, Sisman, Gordon, McCormick, Hamilton, Archibald, Broome. Subs, Hampson I, McClelland I, McClelland II, Goodeve, Peace, Thomson I, Hollinger I, Davis, Cockfield.

Pickering—Henderson, Williams, Creed, Craig, Hay, Lanier, Phipps, Terry, Glendenning, Franssi, Straus, Rogers. Subs, Thompson, Milligan, Todd, Myers.

Seconds versus Lakefield, 1937.

THIRD TEAM FOOTBALL

Coached by Mr. Smith, and captained by Sisman, the Thirds had a successful season, winning games from Appleby II and T.C.S. III, but losing to Mr. Little's 135 pound U.C.C. team. At the beginning of the season the tackling was weak and ball-handling erratic, but some improvement was made as the short season advanced. As a team we were proud of our *esprit de corps*. The Thirds played later than any Upper School team, having its last fixture in the rain against Upper Canada on November 13th. No opposing team carried the ball over our touch line; any touch-down scored against us was from a fumble—not that such a record deserves much credit; we did work at times, however, to maintain it. We were proud, too, to have the privilege of filling up the Second Team ranks in their final game against Pickering Juniors.

We take off our hats to the U.C.C. team that beat us. They were smaller, but better.

For the Thirds everybody played well, and to commend any individuals might be unfair. At that risk, however, we record that on the line Cockfield and McClelland II performed well; in the backfield Peace was reliable and effective, Hamilton showed speed when he got away, Cockfield kicked well.

The following were awarded Third Football Colours: Broome, Cockfield, Davis, Goodeve, Hamilton I, Hampson I, Hollinger I, McClelland I, McClelland II, Peace, Roscoe, Sisman, Thomson I.

THIRD RUGBY TEAM
First Row—Left to Right—D M. McClelland, D. I. A. Thomson, J. G. McClelland, J. E. Sisman, H. K. Hamilton, G. D. Peace. W. G. Goodeve.
Second Row—Left to Right—J. E. Davis, D. E. J. Hampson, R. M. Broome, R. L. Roscoe, B. E. Hollinger. A. S. Cockfield.
Third Row—Left to Right—G. W. Smith Esq., K. F. MacLaren, A. S. Rutter, A. C. Ericson.

Thirds against Appleby II

The opening Third Team game was played on Tuesday, October 26th, at Appleby. The play was fast though erratic, and the score was 14-1 in our favour at full time.

In the opening quarter S.A.C., defending the south end of the field, received the kick-off and made yards several times on plunges and end runs. Cockfield kicked behind Appleby's line where McClelland I dropped on a fumbled ball for the opening tally of the game. Davis's convert went neatly between the posts to make the quarter-time score 6-0 for us.

In the second quarter St. Andrew's resorted to kicking, and the Appleby team was kept in its end of the field; their kicking kept our backs busy. Carrying the ball to Appleby's one yard line, the Saints failed to major. Cockfield kicked for two points on rouges. In this quarter McClelland II's bucking kept us well in the enemy territory.

The third quarter had barely opened when Thomson I was rouged behind the Red and White line for Appleby's lone point. Appleby resorted to repeated forward passes, and brought the ball dangerously near our goal line. McClelland I, however, intercepted one and ran the ball out of the danger zone. The score at three-quarter time remained 8-1.

Both teams started hard in the last quarter, but the play was ragged, and fumbles were costly to each side. Thomson I went through the Appleby line for 10 yards, immediately following which Hamilton received a forward pass and ran 60 yards for a touchdown, which Davis converted for the last point of the game. Score: S.A.C. III 14, Appleby II, 1.

St. Andrew's Thirds—Sisman, Broome, Peace, Hamilton, Thomson I, Goodeve, McClelland I, McClelland II, Hampson I, Cockfield, Hollinger I, Davis.

T.C.S. III's vs. S.A.C. III's

The Thirds journeyed to Port Hope for their second encounter of the season, on Friday, Oct. 29th, to play T.C.S. III's. With a soggy field and frequent showers, the play was at times ragged.

S.A.C. elected to kick off in the first quarter. S.A.C. stopped their heavier opponents on their forty yard line, coming dangerously near to pushing it over. The T.C.S. line held but Cockfield kicked a rouge for the opening point of the game. Several minutes later another rouge was added, bringing the score to 2-0. A determined T.C.S. team drove the Red and White back to their twenty-five yard line, where Peace broke through, eluding all players for a major score. It was converted by Davis. Score at the end of first quarter was 8-0.

The second quarter opened with plenty of line bucks by both sides. McClelland II plunged through for a fifteen yard gain, Goodeve adding another fifteen yards on a cut-back. Hamilton broke away around the right end for thirty yards and a touchdown. The convert was blocked, and the quarter ended 13-0.

Holding grimly to their lead S.A.C. redoubled their efforts, and by extension plays, cutbacks and end runs, finally brought the ball to T.C.S.'s five yard line, with Sisman plunging it over. The convert was again blocked. A redoubled effort on the part of T.C.S., together with a rather hasty aerial attack proved to no avail, the score remaining 18-0 at the end of the third quarter.

Hamilton broke away early in the final quarter, for an end run to the right, and went across the touch line standing up. The convert was blocked, and no further scoring by either team broke the 24-0 victory when the final whistle blew. Hamilton, McClelland II, and Peace, played well for the Saints, with Thompson starring for T.C.S.

T.C.S.—Le Mesurier, Alexander, Ross, Jemmett, Lebrovey, Hyndman, Landrey, Cartwright, Thompson, Giffen, Hart.

S.A.C.—Goodeve, McClelland I, McClelland II, Hollinger I, Cockfield, Davis, Hampson, Thomson, Peace, Hamilton, Broome, Sisman. Subs, Rutter, Maclaren, Roscoe.

U.C.C. 135 LBS. VS. S.A.C. III's

The Thirds were handed their first setback of the season by a U.C.C. 135 lb. team in Toronto, Wednesday, Nov. 3rd.

With a high wind behind them, U.C.C. kicked off in the first quarter, stopping Thomson on the thirty yard line. Plunging for two downs for a no yard gain, Jarvis of U.C.C. kicked a high drifting ball, which Thomson fumbled behind the line for a five point loss. St. Andrew's kept the ball in enemy territory, only to be driven back on the kick. Another fumble behind the line proved costly for S.A.C., with the convert ending the first quarter, U.C.C. leading 12-0.

S.A.C., favoured with the wind in the second quarter, started an aerial attack, with a completed pass from Thomson to McClelland I netting a twenty yard gain. Sisman and Broome plunged deep into the U.C.C. defence, but failed to put it across the line. Cockfield opened the scoring for S.A.C. with a rouge before the quarter time whistle.

Once again hampered by the wind, the Saints kept to plunges and end runs, with Hollinger I smashing through for substantial yardage, enabling McClellanl I to score on a cutback; Davis converted. Jarvis' punting drove S.A.C. back to their twenty-five yard line, with a well placed field goal making the score 15-7.

The Thirds failed to take advantage of the wind in the last quarter, although the play was wide open. Hampson's passing took S.A.C. up the field, but Taylor carried the ball back for forty yards and a rouge. Despite a concerted attempt to regain the lost yardage, S.A.C. were held in their own quarter, with another rouge by U.C.C. cinching the game. Cockfield,

Davis, and Peace turned in good performances, although the final score ended 7-17.

U.C.C. 135—Taylor, Jarvis, Hodgson, Meredith, Grofan, Heintzman, Campbell, Wilson, Gibson, Busk, Northwood.

S.A.C. III's—McClelland I, McClelland II, Hollinger I, Thomson I, Sisman, Hamilton, Peace, Broome, Davis, Cockfield, Hampson, Goodeve.

T.C.S. III's vs. S.A.C. III's

On Saturday, Nov. 6th, S.A.C. III's again defeated T.C.S. III's at Aurora in a hard-fought, well earned match, by the score of 10-0. T.C.S., out to revenge their former licking, provided stiff opposition during the whole game.

S.A.C. kicked off to T.C.S., who took their first down on their forty yard line. Owing to a fumble, the Saints received their first down inside the T.C.S. zone. Failing to make a touch, Cockfield kicked a rouge to open the scoring. T.C.S. were held in their own territory while Cockfield had time to score another rouge.

T.C.S. began to open up, with plenty of end runs in the second quarter. S.A.C. promptly retaliated by bottling up the plays, and camping in T.C.S. territory. Davis placed a well-directed field goal between the uprights to raise the score to 5-0. McClelland I and Goodeve, in wing positions, tackled well to avert any end runs from materializing.

A concerted drive up field by T.C.S. placed them on the Saints' five yard line, but Thomson I recovered a fumbled ball to place it out of the danger zone. The soggy field was fairly well torn up in the third quarter, allowing no sharp twisting or dodging. Hamilton, carrying the ball, was downed by the remaining T.C.S. fullback after a forty-five yard sprint. No score in this quarter.

Backed by a solid line, and the plunging of Hampson and Hollinger, S.A.C. moved towards the T.C.S. goal line. Davis' blocking on the line enabled S.A.C. to stay fairly close to the T.C.S. touch zone. A completed Hampson to Goodeve pass brought the Thirds close enough, for McClelland II and Cockfield to open a hole through which Sisman plunged to make the score 10-0, the convert being blocked. Irwin and Thompson starred for T.C.S., while Thomson I, Davis, and Cockfield led the Saints to victory.

S.A.C. III—Goodeve, McClelland I, McClelland II, Hollinger I, Cockfield, Davis, Hampson I, Thomson I, Peace, Hamilton, Broome, Sisman. Subs, Rutter, Maclaren, Roscoe.

T.C.S.—Le Mesurier, Alexander, Ross, Jemmett, Lebrovey, Hyndman, Landry, Cartwright, Thompson, Giffen, Hart, Waters.

S.A.C. THIRDS VS. U.C.C. 135 LB. TEAM

On Saturday, Nov. 13th, S.A.C. Thirds were defeated by an Upper Canada 135 lb. team at Aurora with a score of 10-0. It rained throughout the game, and the field was very slippery, resulting in several fumbles by both teams.

S.A.C. kicked off and on gaining possession of the ball shortly after, threw a pass which was intercepted by U.C.C. who kicked for a rouge.

Early in the second quarter U.C.C. kicked for another point and managed to block a kick and fall on the ball well in S.A.C. territory. They manoeuvred the ball into position, and kicked a placement for an additional three points. S.A.C. managed to buck the ball to the U.C.C. 20 yard line but a fumble gave the ball to the visitors. The score at half time was U.C.C. 5, S.A.C. 0.

U.C.C. received the kick off, moved the ball up the field and attempted a rouge which they barely failed to get due to some fine running by Hamilton of S.A.C., The score at three quarter time was unchanged.

In the last quarter, long runs for U.C.C. by Taylor and later Jarvis brought the visiting team to the Saints' 2 yard line. They failed to get the touchdown, but a subsequent fumble by S.A.C. behind their own line gave them another five points. The touch was unconverted. The score at the end of the game was 10-0 for U.C.C.

Cockfield kicked consistently and Peace played well for S.A.C., while Jarvis was the star for U.C.C.

U.C.C. 135 lb. Team—Jarvis, Taylor, Heintzman, Busk, Calhoun, Gibson, Little, Rathgeb, Meredith, Northwood, Gedson, Gurble, Wilson, Aird, Campbell, Graham, Ridler, T. Mills, J. L. Mills.

S.A.C.—McClelland I, Hampson I, Cockfield,. Hollinger I, McClelland II, Davis, Goodeve, Thomson I, Peace, Hamilton, Broome, Sisman.

FOURTH TEAM RUGBY

This year for the first time in several, a Third Squad was formed. Mr. Millward and Mr. O'Brian coached us. Hampson II ended up as Fourth team captain. The squad above us was theoretically to create the third and fourth teams,—we, the Fifth. Soon, however, the Third Team became a business-like machine, leaving their scrubs rather disorganized; we accordingly usurped the names "Fourth" and "Fifth" and enticed a few scrubs from the squad above us. We had much fun and managed to get six games: two each with Appleby, Pickering, and T.C.S. There were four wins and two losses. (Don't worry if you find some names on both the Fourth and Fifth Teams.) After the Fifth's game with Appleby we were asked to strengthen our team which we did by adding three or four boys. We now called ourselves the Fourth's. By the end of the season the team was playing very well,—for example: we were able to turn the tables on T.C.S. Littlesides from a 40-1 defeat to a 13-12 victory in the return match. It is hoped that the fundamentals of football learned this year will percolate upwards through the school with us and maybe stand the school in good stead in the near future.

FOURTH RUGBY TEAM
First Row—Left to Right—C. J Higgs, W. M. McPherson, D. B. Kilpatrick, L. G. Hampson, D. H. Gurton, F. H. Hopkins, G. C. Morlock.
Second Row—Left to Right—V. J. Diver, F. A. Diver, John Bryan, J. C. Macorra, K. M. Johnston, W. J. Shields, C. D. MacIntosh.
Third Row—Left to Right—G. S. O'Brian Esq., W. G. Dean, G. M. Frost, W. G. Buchanan, R. S. Sheppard Jr., R. M. Doggett, J. B. Millward Esq.

The following were awarded Fourth Colours: Hampson II (captain), Diver I, Diver II, Gurton, Higgs, Hopkins, Johnston II, Kilpatrick I, MacIntosh II, McPherson, Morlock, Tisdall.

Fourth Team at T.C.S. Littlesides

Appleby having generously asked us to strengthen our Fifths, we added two or three players and called the team the "Fourths". As games had been arranged with T.C.S. and Pickering for this team, it was kept intact for the rest of the season. The first game was on October 29th at Port

Hope against Trinity Littlesides; we lacked organization, and were badly beaten 40 to 1.

T.C.S. were much faster, and ran around our ends repeatedly. The score at half-time was 20 to 0 against us. We had hopes of scoring in the third quarter after repeated plunges by Higgs had taken the ball to Trinity's ten yard line. There, however, we fumbled, and T.C.S. recovered. They continued to pile up the score chiefly by some fine running by Higginbotham. Kilpatrick kicked St. Andrew's only point, after Diver II gained ground on a long forward pass.

Higginbotham scored six touchdowns for T.C.S. and played a fine game.

S.A.C. Fourths—Hampson II, Gurton, Johnston II, Kilpatrick I, Bryan, Diver I, Diver II, Higgs, Morlock, Tisdall, McPherson, Hopkins, Dean, Shields, MacIntosh II, Good, Wilson, Johnson I.

T.C.S. Littlesides—Higginbotham, Cleland, Sommerville, Cayley I, Cayley II, Duggan II, Rougvie, Lambert, Black, Langdon, Finley, O'Hanlon, Holton, Tate, Redpath, Beardshaw.

FOURTHS AGAINST PICKERING AT NEWMARKET

On November 4th the Fourth Team went to Pickering College whom they defeated 10-6. They appeared slightly lighter than we did when the teams took the field, although some of their smaller boys didn't play much. Both teams played good football.

S.A.C. had the wind for the first quarter, and Kilpatrick soon kicked behind the Pickering line where Johnston II fell on a loose ball for a touch. It was unconverted. In the second period the Fourths plunged more, Higgs making excellent gains. Shortly before half-time Higgs carried the ball through their left centre about ten yards for our second touchdown. The score was 10-0 for S.A.C. at half-time.

We left Higgs on the side-line in the second half as he was thought to be too tall, and we missed him. The third quarter opened with Gurton recovering a Pickering fumble near their end, but S.A.C. were unable to capitalize on it. Pickering played up well in the second half; they kicked well; our backs fumbled sometimes, and Pickering made yards through the line. Before the end of the game Pickering carried over a touchdown and converted it. The final score was S.A.C. 10, Pickering 6, and the latter were pressing when the whistle blew.

S.A.C.—Hampson II, Gurton, Kilpatrick, Bryan, Johnston II, Diver I, Diver II, Tisdall, Hopkins, McPherson, Shields, Dean, Higgs, MacIntosh II, Johnson II, Good.

Pickering—Apple, Beer, Brantford, Davis, Dorland, Henery, Mays, Mutch, Meeld, Ballard, Frost, Williamson, Lawson, McNally, Roberts, Rankine I, Rankine II.

S.A.C. Fourths vs. T.C.S. Littleside at Aurora, November 6th

Having been thoroughly trounced at Port Hope on October 29th, our Fourth Team worked very hard towards the return game and turned the tables by a close victory, 13 to 12, at Aurora on November 6th. T.C.S. were weakened somewhat by Cleland's absence from their backfield, but Higginbotham, who scored 6 touchdowns against us in the first game, was unable to escape the S.A.C. tackling.

Both teams played good football; Hampson II handled our team excellently, and the S.A.C. tackling was really good. Sommerville scored all the T.C.S. points; the game must have been a good one, for his picture was in the Toronto *Telegram,*—and rightly so.

First quarter: field goal by Sommerville, kick into touch by Sommerville. Second quarter: rouge for S.A.C. off Kilpatrick's punt, touchdown for S.A.C. by Johnston II who intercepted a forward pass and dodged twenty yards for a touchdown which Kilpatrick converted. Half-time score: S.A.C. 7, T.C.S. 4.

Third quarter: field goal for T.C.S. by Sommerville, rouge for S.A.C., touchdown for S.A.C. when Higgs bucked over. Fourth quarter: touchdown for T.C.S. by Sommerville from a forward pass twenty-five yards out in the clear. Final score: S.A.C. 13, T.C.S. 12.

Everybody played well on both teams; Sommerville starred for T.C.S.; Kilpatrick's kicking and Higgs' plunging helped S.A.C.

St. Andrew's Fourths—Hampson II, Gurton, Johnston II, Kilpatrick I, Bryan, Diver I, Diver II, Higgs, Morlock, Tisdall, MacPherson, Hopkins, Dean, Shields, MacIntosh II, Flemming, Good.

Trinity Littlesides—Higginbotham, Duggan II, Sommerville, Hart II, Cayley I, Cayley II, Rougvie, Lambert, Black, Langdon, Finley, O'Hanlon, Holton, Tate, Redpath, Beardshaw.

Fifths at Appleby Thirds

The Fifths played their first game against Appleby Thirds at Oakville on October 20th, and showed the effect of the late school opening in a lack of cohesion and confidence which cost them an 18-0 defeat. Appleby Thirds were in this game superior, to a degree greater than might have been justified by their slightly heavier team.

In the first half Calverly twice tackled for rouges, Dowding kicked to the deadline and Macbeth scored an unconverted touch after intercepting one of our forward passes. We made yards several times, but often lost the ball on fumbles. In the second half we were unable to wipe out any of this; Beardmore scored another touch for Appleby and Walsh tackled Shields for another rouge. Although our team finished trying hard, and were in a position to score in the last quarter, they failed to score. Appleby tackled well. They were good hosts, and we all enjoyed the game. We thought

FIFTH RUGBY TEAM
First Row—Left to Right—J. R Crowe, J. E. Kilmer, J. R. Good, W. A. Cobban, W. A. Lofft, R. H. Rolph, R. A. Merner.
Second Row—Left to Right—M. T. Wilson, D. S. Garraway, C. H. Heintzman, J. H. Johnson, L. A. Lillico, D. P. Flemming.
Third Row—Left to Right—G. S. O'Brian Esq., W. G. Buchanan, J. B. Millward Esq.

they were good sports to ask us to put on some bigger boys for the return match.

S.A.C.—Shields, Hampson II, Bryan, Lofft, Diver II, Kilmer, Hemming, Tisdall, Johnson I, Johnson II, Morlock, Doggett, Heintzman, MacIntosh II, Cobban, Ellis.

Appleby—Beardmore, Surtzer, Macbeth, McGuire, Dowding, Pearce, Wilson, Silverthorn, Walsh, Davis, Calverley, Stalker, Jackson, Huston, **Tizard**.

On Wednesday, October 27th, the Third Appleby team came to St. Andrew's. The St. Andrew's team, however, outplayed the Oakville team and won by a score of 21-11 in a hard fought game. Higgs played well for St. Andrew's and Johnson II did fine running. Dowding kicked well for Appleby, obtaining six points for his side. The Appleby touchdown was scored by Calverley on a fumble behind the St. Andrew's line. The line ups for the teams were:

Appleby—Stalker, Calverley, Silverthorne, Wilson, Pearce, Ingles, Jackson, MacBeth, Walsh, Switzer, Dowding. Subs, Heuston, McGuire.

S.A.C.—Hampson II, Diver II, MacIntosh II, Morlock, Kilmer, Higgs, Johnson II, Gurton, Flemming, Bryan, Johnson I, Tisdall. Subs, Shields, Heintzman I.

Rugby Sevens and Soccer Sixes

The object of the intramural athletic programme is to enable every boy to play as a member of some team and to provide competition, rather than to declare champions. The entire programme was very successfully organized and supervised by the boys.

The Upper School was divided into teams for Rugby Sevens. The games were played under C.R.U. rules, except that seven boys constituted a team; wide-open rugby football was featured. Seaton's *Lanarks* and O'Brian's *Selkirks* were undefeated when weather conditions interrupted the play-off. Other teams in the League were *Fyfes, Ayrs,* and *Argylls,* captained by Christie, Bonnell, and Macdonald; respectively.

The Middle School was organized into four Soccer Sixes: *Dornochs* (Diver I), *Kilmarnocks* (Shields),—*Lothians* (Kilpatrick I) and *Orkneys* (Morlock). The play was fast and hard. When the schedule was over the *Dornochs* led by a wide margin.

Although the general idea of the post-football-season Rugby Sevens and Soccer Sixes was the fun of playing, the games were all very keenly contested.

Rugby Sevens—Tied for First Place—*Selkirks*—O'Brian (captain), Macrae, Hollinger II, Langelier, Senior, Cockfield, Goodeve, Maclaren. *Lanarks*—Seaton (captain), Kent, Knight, Rogers, Gordon, Davison, Sisman, Roscoe.

Soccer Sixes—Winners—*Dornochs*—Diver I (captain), Tisdall, Macorra, Frost, Crowe, Gurton, Kilmer, Heintzman, Willis.

The Cross-Country Run

An outstanding event of the year was the Senior cross-country run, which took place Wednesday, November the 17th. A total of sixty-two boys started. At the sound of the gun a few sprang to the fore in an attempt to gain the bridge, one of the most notable spurts of speed being exhibited by Mitchell. Before the long line of struggling contestants was out of sight of the college, Bonnell, exhibiting his true form, took the lead which he held to the end. When the leaders were nearing the farthest point in the course, a violent but soon-spent hail storm occurred which failed to dampen the spirit of the runners. Towards the end Bonnell widened the gap, and finished in 22.57 minutes, only 1.13 minutes over the standing record. Good time considering the slippery and muddy course. Thompson and Senior, coming next, were running very evenly, but on the sprint Senior lost to Thompson, who crossed the line a few inches ahead.

Approximately fifteen minutes later the rear guard streaked across the finishing line. For obvious reasons, the names (one being the writer's) will be withheld.

That afternoon the awards were presented by Mrs. O'Brian. Bonnell received the gold medal, Thompson the silver, and Senior the bronze. The remainder of the awards were cakes donated by the masters, presented to the respective winners, the prefects receiving the majority. These awards were as follows: Macdonald, who came fifth, the prefects' cake; O'Brian, who came in sixth place, the first football squad; Roscoe, coming fourth, the second squad; Shields, coming sixteenth, the third squad; Rogers, who came eighth, the Flavelle House; Christie, running eleventh, the Memorial House, and Merner for the Upper Sixth, Davidson for the Lower Sixth, Diver Primus for the Fifth Form, and Rutter for the Fourth Form.

FARRER

SWIMMING

The swimming programme started the last week in November, and will run on until late in January. As the major part of the competitions we shall be having take place after the Christmas holiday, and as the date for the printer comes rather early, it has been decided to publish a full account of the Swimming Team's record in the next number. Meets have been arranged with the Ontario Agricultural College, the University of Western Ontario Freshman, and arrangements are pending for a meet with Trinity College School.

62   St. Andrew's College Review

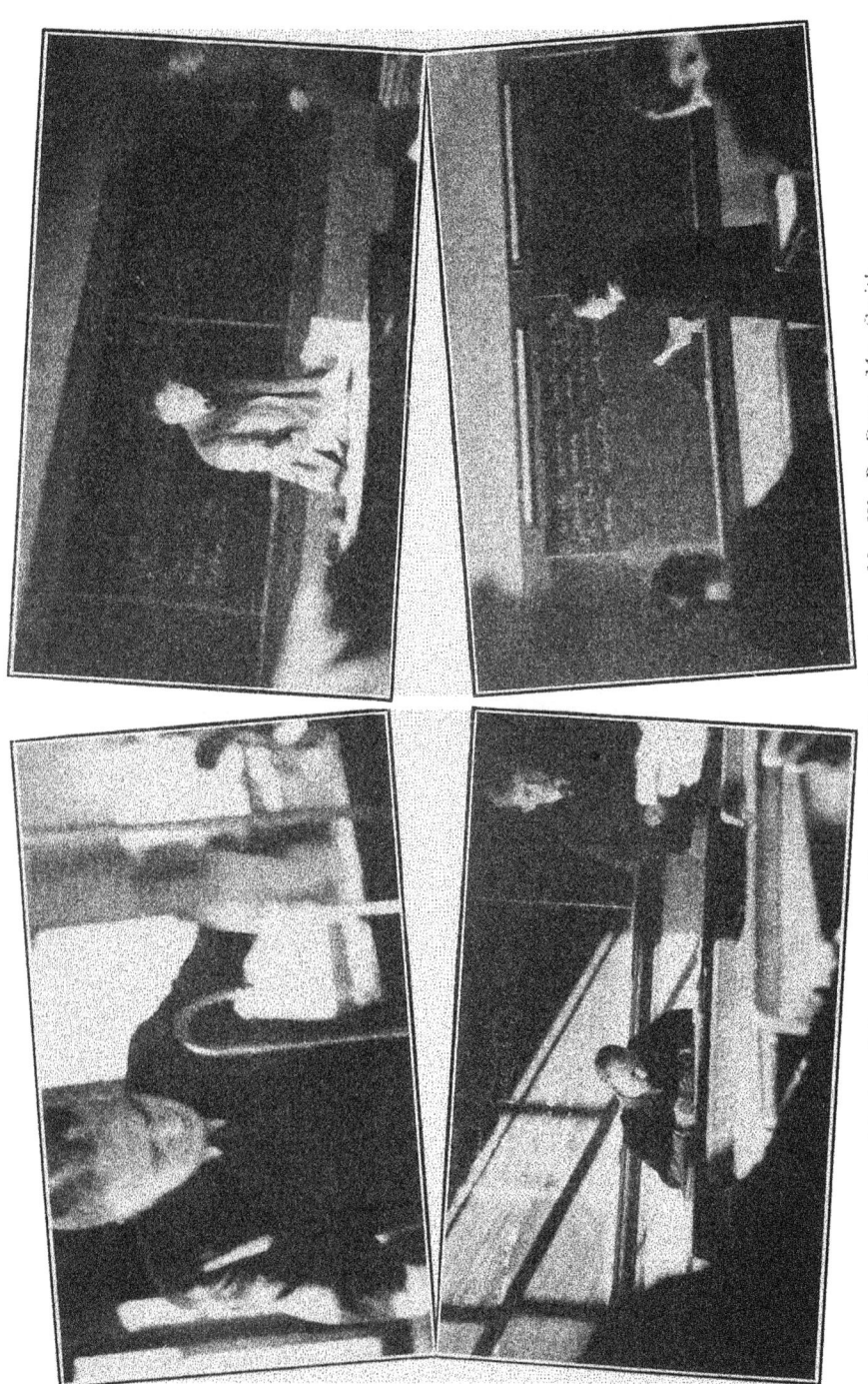

Masters taken unaware, left to right, Mr. Goodman, Mr. W. B. Ross, Mr. Smith, Mr. O'Brien. "And why weren't you paying attention to your work, Heintzman?"

The personnel is showing promise under Mr. Griffith's coaching. The services of Wadds, and also Howe and Finley—all on last year's team—will be greatly missed.　　　　　　　　　　　　　　　　M.G.K.

BASKETBALL

Both Swimming and Basketball take a position in the college games programme minor to Football, Hockey, and Cricket. Much enthusiasm has been shown however this fall, and the season opened earlier than usual. As is the case with Swimming, the Basketball season extends well into next term, necessitating a postponement of publication, until our next issue, of a complete record.

Macdonald I is again captain. Macdonald, Seaton and Knight have been doing fine work so far; Grass and Knight, who were alternates last year, deserve places on the first line as guards. Kilpatrick I and Davis, who are new to the team, are playing great basketball, as are the other alternates: Macdonald II, Cockfield and Kent.

So far three games have been played, of which two were won and one was lost. The Aurora High School, playing after less practice than we had had, lost to us by a wide margin. It was rather an easy game, and we had the advantage of height. We beat Pickering in a game in which Macdonald, Seaton and Knight, did most of the scoring. At the time of going to press, our last game has been played against a mixed team from the Ontario Agricultural College who beat us by a very close score. Although the Aggies were slow in starting, they turned out to be a faster and probably superior team. We managed, however, to do very well against them particularly as Seaton, the forward spark-plug that day, retired early in the game with a "charlie horse".

Under the continued able coaching of Mr. Millward we hope to develop into a better team as the season advances.

　　　　　　　　　　　　　　　　　　　　　　　　　　　M.G.K.

Mr. Musgrove has been coaching a junior basketball squad which has been practising hard, but about which it is so far impossible to give accurate information. The boys are keen but inexperienced. When the season is over, your basketball reporter will collate all information about all the teams and dish it up for the Summer Number.

　　　　　　　　　　　　　　　　　　　　　　　　　　　B.B.

Far Across The Waters

Far across the waters, where the Alpine rivers flow,
Sit agéd men, from all the lands; for why, we do not know.
They say they settle wars and debts, and in the nick of time
Suppress the tyrants of the land, and free the world from crime.

But far across the waters, these men just sit and think,
And when the trouble rises, they take another drink.
One member old and sleepy, hard his nose he blew:
"I hear that 'Mussy's' arming, forsooth what shall we do?"

Now far across the waters, another yawned and said:
"I vote we let 'em fight it out, for soon they'll all be dead."
"Nay, nay, my friends; let's linger and order up more rye,
For after that we'll all be fit, this matter well to try."

Still far across the waters, another year's gone by
And all the sages of the League are tossing down more rye.
The war's still on, and many more have risen and died out.
Yet there across the waters, these men still drink and shout.

D. G. M.

Editor's Note. We publish this contribution "without recourse"; we refuse to be sued by the League of Nations. As a matter of fact, the contributor may be wrong. For example, we understand rye to be a sort of Canadian national drink, and that at Geneva they drink scotch and vodka.

Macdonald House

Front door, Macdonald House, and some of this term's tenants.

THE BEAGLE HUNT

Much to the joy of the new boys, but not quite so much of the old boys a Beagle Hunt was held on the afternoon of Thursday, November 11th. This day (Armistice) being a half-holiday it was quite befitting to follow the hounds. A great crowd assembled on the ploughed field behind the power-house and the Hunt began. For the first mile or so, it was uneventful; but at about a half-mile on the other side of Bathurst Street the Beagles scented a hare and gave chase, tearing back in the opposite direction. After several hours of pursuing them, and finding it a fruitless hope to catch up to them, the boys gave it up, and departed for the school after a very happy but exhausting afternoon.

J.R.M.K.

LOWER SCHOOL DINING-ROOM

This year our own dining-room, which for the last seven years has lain idle, was reopened and a new staff organized. In the previous years, we have had to walk over to the Upper School Dining-Room whether it be raining, snowing, hailing or thundering. We are, therefore, very pleased with this new arrangement, for not only is this new "Munch Hall" closer to us, but the rising bell is rung fifteen minutes later this year. Miss De Vigne is supplying us with excellent victuals but there is not enough ice cream.

J.R.M.K.

By Rapmund, Form I.

MACDONALD HOUSE PLAYROOM

The Macdonald House Playroom or Ping Pong room has, for the last few years lain idle. But under the leadership of Mr. Macrae the boys have hopes of repairing this room. The changes which it will undergo, in the end, we are sure, will make it a bright spot in the life of Macdonald House. After the room has been repainted and furnished it will make a very nice room. We have hopes that the room will be ready for use at the beginning of next term. If so, it will have a formal opening and will be used during the boys leisure time. The furnishings will be as follows: One or two Ping Pong tables (two most likely), one game of shuffle board, one small billiard table, several games of chess and checkers and various other games contributed by the boys themselves. We are at present decorating the room and are looking forward to this new pleasure next term.

THE WARDENS AND LIBRARIANS

The Macdonald House wardens are this year—Graham and Cameron II. The latter is also Captain of the First Lower School Rugby Team and Second Form representative to the Athletic Association.

The librarians this year are—Kilpatrick II and Cody.

ARTS AND CRAFTS

The "Arts and Crafts" department is this year under the care of Mr. Macrae. The boys in the Lower School from Upper II down are enjoying this privilege very much. Although work has not yet begun on a large scale, it is hoped that shortly some specimens of MacDonald House skill will be forthcoming. The woodcraft room is filled with boys who, under the guidance of Mr. (Charlie) Badger, the carpenter, have produced various clever and useful articles.

Last year, when there was no Saturday morning school, this work was voluntary; now that we have classes on these days, arts and crafts are carried on as part of the regular school work. The boys have high hopes for future success in these rooms which are usually full at all times. Mr. Macrae who is in charge, is also very clever in this hobby.

ART

Mr. Ives has taken charge of the art classes. He is, himself, very good at drawing and painting. Last year, Mr. Dowden had charge of a small art class which this year has developed into a regular subject held during school hours. We hope that this class may thrive and are very grateful to Mr. Ives for taking charge of it.

SOAP CARVING

With the arrival of Mr. Ives a new hobby has entered the Lower School, namely soap carving. Our new master is very clever in this art. The boys have taken it up very eagerly, and are producing some remarkable specimens. These weird objects are becoming more perfect, and a few of them are beginning to resemble various animals. There has been a heavy boom on soap, and Miss De Vigne has been kept very busy supplying us with soap for carving purposes. However, the St. Andrew's boys are also in the habit of using soap for cleansing purposes, that is, most of them. The carving designs are taken from a small booklet which Mr. Ives lent us. Some of the carvings are very good, while others are not; and to determine who was the best soap-carver, a competition was arranged. All competitors had to do everything themselves and could get no assistance from a master or boy. As a result of this announcement, a great number of exhibits were handed in and were judged by Mrs. Tudball, who after a long period of examination, pronounced a "whippet", done by J. H. Cody, the best carving. A model of a Dutch boy came second, done by Stappels.

The boys were well pleased by the results and we all have great hopes for the continuation of this interesting hobby.

J.R.M.K.

Macdonald House Rugby

The Macdonald House team this year was on the whole very successful. Mr. Macrae was coach again, and he has trained the team till it reached a high pitch. Although the term was shortened considerably by our late start, players were quickly sorted out, and the season began. Mr. Macrae had the team on the new field behind the tennis courts, practising every afternoon. The weather being fine, the first squad would assemble at 3.30 P.M. and practice till 5.00 P.M. The following boys received colours:

Graham, Augustine, Butler, Sabiston, Cameron II, captain; Pollock, Pilley, Fraser, Jolliffe, Mitchell, Silliman.

There were four games played and St. Andrew's won three of them losing only to the Christ Church team.

J.R.M.K.

First Lakefield Game

The first game of the season was held on October 27th, when the team went to Lakefield Preparatory School. It was a very good game, and both teams did very well. In the first half S. A. C. kicked off and the Lakefield man was downed by Butler. There was some excellent interference in our line. Broken field running by Mitchell proved successful, and Fraser's plunging was spectacular. It is unjust to pick out the best players in the game; although some running was very colourful, most of it was made possible by the splendid work of the line. Mitchell out-kicked his opponent, and his forward passes were usually caught by Pollock. The Grove put up a fine show; Vaughan and Coldwell (the latter made their touchdown) were the best for Lakefield, Vaughan bearing the brunt of most of the tackling. In the first half, the Lakefield forward passes were a treat, but they were soon checked, and the final score turned out to be: MacDonald House, 37; Lakefield, 5.

MACDONALD HOUSE RUGBY TEAM
First Row—Left to Right—C. B. Pollock, W. B. Butler, A. F. Moss, K. G. Cameron, D. P. Sabiston, R. L. Graham, K C. Pilley.
Second Row—Left to Right—T. B. D. Tudball Esq., H. B. Mitchell, J. D. Fraser, D. B. Silliman, R. S. Jolliffe, J. M. Macrae Esq.
Third Row—Left to Right—T. R. Hastings, R. B. Stapells, D. G. Cameron.

The teams were as follows:

S. A. C.—Snap, Graham; Insides, Moss, Augustine; Middles, Butler, Sabiston; Outsides, Pollock, Pilley; Quarter, Cameron II; Halves, Fraser, Jolliffe, Silliman, Mitchell.

The Grove—Snap, Gunn; Insides, Andrews, Morris; Middles, Wishart, Arnold; Outsides, Vaughan, Pope; Quarter, Harris; Halves, Tilley, Wilkes, Caldwell, Hague.

SECOND LAKEFIELD GAME

The second game was played at St. Andrew's on November 3rd. It was a return game with the Grove. S. A. C. showed great skill in tackling, and by their splendid interference held back their opponents. In the first quarter Lakefield gained ground, but a fumble gave the ball to S. A. C. who carried it down to the five yard line whence Fraser carried it over the line for a touchdown, converted by Mitchell making the score 6-0 for S. A. C. In the second quarter S. A. C. was hard pressed, and at half-time were on their ten yard line. The third quarter was hard fought. Excellent bucks by Fraser, Sabiston and Jolliffe kept up our end. St. Andrew's fumbled at their twenty-five yard line but prevented L. P. S. from gaining ground. In the last quarter S. A. C. showed excellent interference, but were forced to their one yard line. Warren II then made a touchdown for Lakefield but failed to convert it. The final score was S. A. C. 6 and L. P. S. 5. The St. Andrew's team was unchanged, but the Lakefield team was heavier than before.

"Hup—One—Two"—Lower School Team.

T. C. S. GAME

The third game was against Trinity College's Sixth Team and was played at S.A.C. on November 13th. The weather was very bad, for a drizzle commenced early in the afternoon. S.A.C. kicked-off and Butler fell on the ball. In this quarter Fraser, Sabiston and Silliman made good runs. S.A.C. fumbled and T.C.S. drove us back. S.A.C. got the ball and Sabiston, after a spectacular run, scored a touchdown which made the score 5-0 in our favour. Plunging by Sabiston and Fraser was very good. Mitchell kicked splendidly throughout the game. There was excellent interference on both teams during the second quarter, and Butler managed to jump on a fumbled ball behind the T.S.C. line making the score 10-0 in our favour. There was no further score throughout the game. Bucking on both sides was very good, and Fraser, Jolliffe and

Butler excelled themselves. S.A.C. line deserves most of the credit for this game. Moss, Pilley and Augustine tackled very well in the line. The final score was 10-0 for S.A.C. Captain Cameron deserves a great deal of credit for the three games in which he led his team to victory.

The Trinity Team was as follows:

Snap, Cayley; Insides, Oakley, Duncanson; Middles, Lawson, Beardshaw; Quarter, Best; Outsides, Wills, Crawford; Halves, Heaven, McIvor, Robertson, Redpath.

Christ Church Game

The last game of the season was played on Saturday, November 20th, against Christ Church of Toronto at St. Andrew's. Though Christ

Killers and Maneaters.

Church was about half the weight of S.A.C. they played a wonderful game beating us 16-11.

In the first quarter, S.A.C. pushed Christ Church back to their twenty-five yard line, where Fraser plunged across the line for a touchdown. Christ Church showed very plucky resistance and their blocking was good. When they got the ball Rawlinson I scored a touchdown after a splendid run of ninety-five yards. The second quarter was hot all the time, and Sabiston finally scored a touchdown which was not converted. The score stood at 10-5 at half-time for S.A.C. The line work of both teams was excellent and Mitchell's kicking splendid. S.A.C. fumbled to lose ten yards but soon recovered them. The S.A.C. line deserves credit for its work in this quarter. The third quarter was the most spectacular of the whole game Christ Church scored two touchdowns, the second one being converted by Bruce Rawlinson. Smith I was responsible for those last two touchdowns and the score stood at 16-10 for Christ Church. In the last quarter, Mitchell kicked over Christ Church line for one point, the final score was Christ Church 16 and S.A.C. 11. The Smith brothers and the Rawlinson brothers were the best for the visiting team, while Mitchell, Fraser, Sabiston, and Butler the best for St. Andrew's. It was a great game and Christ Church played a splendid game.

The Rugby season was altogether a success and we all congratulate Mr. Macrae for the fine team he put on the field.

J.R.M.K.

Lower School Senior Squad ready to go to work.

THE KILLERS AND THE MAN-EATERS

This year, two of the most terrific battles ever fought on the gridiron were held on November 5th and 9th respectively. Two teams were chosen from the scrubs of Macdonald House, and named accordingly "The Kilpatrick Killers" and "The Meredith Man Eaters." Mr. Ives and Mr. Macrae officiated.

The first game was on the whole very exciting, and in the first half the "Killers" were in the lead by 5-0. The Man-Eaters made up for this in a short time, after a series of spectacular plunges by Grant and Meredith; the latter purred over the "Killers" line during the last two minutes of play. Captain Meredith then proceeded to convert the touchdown in the last fifteen seconds, by a plunge through the centre of the anguished "Killers." The game was very close, and Meredith deserves credit for his dogged and successful plunges. Mrs. Tudball who announced that two cakes would be given to the winning team, presented them in the library.

The second game was equally exciting, and both teams excelled themselves in blocking and plunging. For the winning team of the second game Dr. MacKenzie of Toronto, presented two cakes, one large one for the winners and one smaller one for the losers. Dr. MacKenzie personally watched both these games, I am sure, with pride, for his son, a half-back, put up a brilliant game. Once again in the first half the "Killers" were ahead by 5-0. In the third quarter they plunged their way down to their opponents line for another touchdown, but the Man-Eaters, mettle was up, and with the greatest fury they bore down on their heavier opponents till they too scored a touchdown. At the last quarter, the score stood at 10-5 in favour of the "Killers." These worthies promptly proceeded to score another touchdown by Hunter. This was the only touchdown that was converted. The Man-Eaters strove furiously to withstand the attack of the "Killers" whose weight was an advantage. The final score stood at 16-5 for the "Killers." The best players of the "Man-Eaters" were Meredith, Grant and Franceschini, and of the "Killers" were MacKenzie, Booth and O'Brien II. Hunter also played a good game.

The cakes were presented by Dr. MacKenzie after the game and victors and vanquished alike were very pleased.

The Changing of the Colours

WE had to rise about seven in the morning in order to see the king of England changing the colours of his regiments.

We went by the underground railway for about ten minutes and eventually emerged at Hyde Park Corner. My father and I walked across the Park and saw people hustling and bustling about the grass—eager to reach the grand stands. Soon we saw a large open space surrounded by huge stands. We came late so were left to stand with the majority of the crowd. Luckily we got a few seats to stand on and were able to see over the heads of the crowd.

Later a man came around and asked us to give him some money for the seats. We gave him a few pennies for which he gave us some tickets. We thought he was a fraud. Seeing that we had some friends with us, we secretly passed our tickets along and the man looked very surprised to see that our friends had tickets.

Suddenly, we heard a moan. I looked around and saw that a man had fainted from the hot sun of this bright morning. A doctor kept the crowd away.

At last, the soldiers began to gather on the field. First, marched the Dragoons; then the Forty-Eighth Highlanders; then the king's Own

Riflemen and lastly a large troop of Busbys. A great cheer arose when the carriages bearing the Royal Family arrived. Following them came the king of England, Edward VIII, riding on a beautiful brown horse. Behind him came the Guard of Honour wearing bright uniforms. The Royal Family sat on a special platform, gaily decorated.

When all the troops were lined up, the king began to speak. We were quite a distance away, so we were only able to catch a few words of what he said. Then the captain of each regiment strode forth and the king presented them their new colours. The bands began to play and the crowd to cheer as the king rode out.

Just after the king had passed through the gate at the corner of the Park, we heard a shot ring out! At once there was a great confusion.

An Unnoticed Corner of the Quadrangle.

People started shouting and trying to find out what had happened. Nobody seemed to know. We made our way as quickly as we could in the direction of the noise. The king had gone, but we saw a police patrol wagon slowly moving out of the dense crowd.

As we wearily trudged homewards, we thought of what an experience we had had that day.

Next morning, we read in our papers that king Edward VIII had been shot at, not more than two hundred yards from where we stood.

JAMES BOOTH, LOWER SECOND

Good for you, Booth, you're about the only help your L. S. Editor had this year.

We're very proud that our 48th Highlanders of Toronto put on such a good show.

EDITOR.

Motherly Care

ALONG a hot and dusty road in Northern India ambled a mother elephant and her child, with their keeper at their heels. The mother was hot and tired, and therefore slightly short-tempered; but the baby elephant frisked around her attempting to start a game. This ill-fated baby had just pulled a bush, with which he meant to strike his mother, when a terrific blow flattened his four legs on the ground and stars flew around his head. He arose with a sheepish look, and from then on was the best of babies.

'Xmas '37

During the course of the day the road became more treacherous as they progressed and at one side it ran along the edge of a sloping precipice. The baby elephant thought this very strange and he proceeded to investigate. At this his mother became greatly alarmed lest her child fall over, rushed to the edge of the road and nosed her squealing offspring away from the cliff's edge. After several such attempts to investigate, and after several severe spankings, the baby elephant crept ahead; when around the corner in front of him he ran to the edge and peered over. At this moment his mother rounded the bend and she let out such a scream of rage that her keeper thought she was mad. The baby elephant was so startled that he lost his balance and went rolling, squealing and bumping down the cliff for about three hundred feet.

On seeing this the keeper was frantic, for it meant hundreds of dollars lost to him. The mother elephant did not wait to count her losses, but rushed to the edge of the cliff, and holding her fore-feet in front of her, slid down the cliff on her tail, after her young elephant. A few minutes later the keeper of the elephants was awakened from his despair by sounds of rolling, grunting and shrill screaming. He arrived at the edge of the cliff in time to see the mother elephant rolling her youngster over and over with her head and eventually they arrived at the top, the mother breathless, the baby frightened.

On arriving at the top the mother promptly seized her child and chastised him with great vigour after which, the unpleasant process being over, the trio proceeded on their way, the baby mumbling in elephant language "live and learn."

J.R.M.K.

THE JUNIOR CROSS-COUNTRY RUN

The annual Junior Cross-Country Run was held on Tuesday, November 16th, at 4.15 p.m. There were forty-five contestants ranging from fifteen years to eight years of age. Mr. Macrae started the race; as the runners swept over the old bridge it tottered and swung. The competitors left the first steward behind, a very bewildered boy The race was fairly close, and the spectators cheered wildly as Brickenden, Hampson II and Williams II swept into view.

The winners of the race were:

1st—Brickenden—Macdonald Cup, and also a silver medal.
2nd—Hampson II—Olympic Shield, and also a bronze medal.

The winners of the cakes were:

First Form Cake—MacKenzie.
Second Form Cake—Williams II.
Third Form Cake—Pollock.
Upper Flat Cake—Mitchell II.
Lower Flat Cake—Franceschini.

After the race, all the boys gathered into the common room of Macdonald House, where Mrs. Tudball presented the prizes and cakes. Mr. Smith, President of the Athletic Association, gave a short address, congratulating the runners and praising the winners. MacDonald I went forward to receive the Steward's cake, leaving the room surrounded by his eager subordinates. The race was altogether a success and everyone was satisfied.

J.R.M.K.

LOWER SCHOOL SKITS

MR. TUDBALL:—"I had a round of golf with my wife this morning, Mr. Macrae."

MR. MACRAE:—"Which won?"

MR. TUDBALL:—"Which one! How many wives do you think I keep?"

* * * *

CANNIBAL:—"Have you anything to say before we eat you?"

KILPATRICK II: (Windy)—"May I be permitted to say a few words on the advantages of vegetarianism?"

The Lion at the Gate.
(Or is it a Wild-cat?)

He had just returned from church, and Mr. Tudball asked, "What was the text of the sermon?"

He answered:—"He giveth his beloved sleep."

MR. TUDBALL:—"Many people there?"

He replied:—"All the beloved."

* * * *

MR. MUSGROVE:—"What are you running away for, Diver?"

DIVER:—"I'm trying to keep two boys from fighting."

MR. MUSGROVE:—"Who are the fellows?"

DIVER:—'Mitchell there,—and me."

* * * *

MR. TUDBALL:—"Come here, Pilley, and tell me what the four seasons are."

PILLEY:—"Pepper, salt, mustard and vinegar."

* * * *

MR. IVES:—"I say, waitress! Remove this cheese quickly."

WAITRESS:—"Isn't it all right, sir?"

MR. IVES:—"Oh, quite all right, it's just eating my bread."

CHARACTER SKETCHES OF MACDONALD HOUSE

	Name	Nickname	Occupation	Ambition	Favourite Sayings
1	D. C. Hunter	"Men"	Being foolish	To get another letter from his cousin Mary	"Lemme alone"
2	R. L. Graham	"Bily"	Sleeping	To get a good sleep to-night	"Yea, Team"
3	A. F. Moss	"Toto"	Making barnyard noises	To make a really funny noise	"You're very unkind to me" "Wee, Wee, Wee, Wee-e-e"!
4	Jen Knox	"Never-Knox"	Fooling with Hunter	To be able to put chalk on Hunter's back, unknown	"Go away, Hunter"
5	Hugh Mitchell	"Spider"	Guzzling in the Tuck-Shop	To cover the warden's mirror with soap again	Eighty cents worth of candy, Mrs. Davis
6	Doug. Fraser	"Phrase"	Trying to act like a movie star	To become a ravishing movie star	"Get out of my way, small fry"
7	G. R. Kilgour	"Gubby"	Trying to be good and innocent	To be 1st in his form all year	I think I passed in this—I think I passed in that, etc.
8	Blackstock	"Skinner"	Nil. (Sleep)	To be a warden	"Go way!" and "What ? ? ?"
9	B uier	"But"	Making lots of noise	To be first in line for hand inspection always	I bought two books,—a Life and a comic magazine.

NEW BOYS

First Row—Left to Right—E. E. Leishman, K. C. Pilley, G. J. Blackstock, J. P. Booth, J. D. Heintzman, F. A. McKenzie, C. W. Eddis, C. B. Pollock, S. D. Carter.
Second Row—Left to Right—A. R. Thiele, G. M. Brickenden, H. B. Mitchell, W. B. Butler, R. S. Jolliffe, J. D. Fraser, W. G. Grant, R. B. Stapells, John Knox, G. R. A. Ramsey.
Third Row—Left to Right—A. S. Rutter, J. R. Good, R. G. Kilgour, F. H. Hopkins, D. S. Garraway, G. A. O'Brian, T. R. Hastings, W. G. Dean, W. G. Goodeve, J. G. McClelland, K. M. Johnston.
Fourth Row—Left to Right—D. H. Gurton, John Bryan, W. A. Lofft, G. M. Frost, R. L. Roscoe, R. S. Sheppard, Maurice Langelier, W. N. McCormick.
Fifth Row—Left to Right—H. H. Davison, G. J. Kinley, J. E. Davis, D. G. Macrae, R. M. Doggett, T. C. Gordon, H. K. Hamilton, W. G. Angus.

MR. MACRAE:—"Brown, you've not done a stroke of work this morning, and I've told you again and again, that the devil will find work for idle hands to do. Now take your copybook and write that out twenty times."

SONS OF OLD BOYS
First Row—Left to Right—C. H. Heintzman, E. E. Leishman, F. A. McKenzie, J. D. Heintzman, G. J. Blackstock, C. D. MacIntosh.
Second Row—Left to Right—A. S. Rutter, R. G. Kilgour, W. M. McPherson, R. L. Graham, T. R. Hastings, H. H. Hamilton, W. H. Diver.
Third Row—Left to Right—J. R. Crowe, J. E. Kilmer, R. H. Rolph, D. P. Flemming, F. A. Diver, V. J. Diver.
Fourth Row—Left to Right—H. H. Davison, Ruliff Grass, D. G. K. MacIntosh, Kenneth Ketchum Esq., K. F. MacLaren, M. G. Kent, H. K. Hamilton.

MR. TUDBALL:—'Now, Mulock, just what passed between yourself and the complainant?'

MULOCK:—"Well, sir, there was two pairs of fists, one turnip, seven bricks, a dozen assorted bad names and a lump of coal; but, of course, I meant no harm."

St. Andrew's College Old Boys' Association

RESOLUTION COMMEMORATING THE PASSING OF
MRS. MACDONALD

At a special General Meeting of the Old Boys Association of St. Andrew's College, held in the Council Chamber of the Board of Trade, Toronto, on Monday, November 29th, 1937, the following resolution was passed:

"The Old Boys of St. Andrew's College share with their former Headmaster, Dr. D. Bruce Macdonald, a deep sense of bereavement in the recent passing of Mrs. Macdonald.

"During thirty-five years Mrs. Macdonald endeared herself to the long succession of boys who have attended St. Andrew's. Her kindly personality and gracious manner were a constant source of strength and inspiration to the Headmaster and of comfort and encouragement to the boys.

"Be it therefore resolved that this Association place on record the profound sorrow with which the Old Boys learned of Mrs. Macdonald's passing.

"And it be it further resolved that a copy of this resolution be forwarded to Dr. Macdonald as an assurance that his great bereavement still further strengthens those bonds of affection and respect which through the years have been forged between him and his Old Boys."

R. ROY MCMURTRY, *President*.
GORDON W. HEWITT, *Secretary*.

Boys who left in June, 1937

Andrew R. Armstrong is attending Meisterschaft and Shaw's in Toronto.

David M. Dickie is in the University of Toronto taking pass Arts. He was playing good football there until a shoulder injury held him up.

Fred Doty is taking an Engineering course at Queen's University.

Warner Eakins has enrolled at McGill, course unknown.

Leighroy Gerhart, who took so many prizes last year, is taking Law at the University of Toronto.

W. Hamilton Grass is taking pass Arts at the University of Toronto, where he played football for Trinity.

William Hees is in business with George Hees, Son & Co.

Donald Hood is working with his father in the paper business.

Arthur R. Kilgour is at the University of Toronto, where he is taking Political Science and Economics.

William King is in the office of the University of Toronto Athletic Association.

Alexander F. McCoubrey is attending North Toronto Collegiate.

Frank F. McEachern is at the University of Toronto taking Arts.

Charles MacIntosh is working in Brampton in the paper business.

Lynden J. Mackey is working in John Anderson's in Lindsay, Ont.

John A. Martin is working with his father in Paris, Ont.

C. Douglas Murray is taking Mining Engineering at Queen's University.

William T. Pentland is in the first year Commerce and Finance at the University of Toronto.

Gibson Phibbs is working with the T. Eaton Company of Toronto.

H. Edwin Roscoe is attending the Michigan College of Mining and Technology.

Charles M. Shields is with Wood, Gundy and Company, Toronto.

Donald Spence is taking honour Philosophy at the University of Toronto.

John B. Spence is attending the Royal Military College in Kingston, where he played quarterback on the first team football.

William B. Wadds is going to the University of Toronto Schools.

1901-06—In May of this year at the American Otological Society, the members elected D. E. Staunton Wishart to the Council of the Society. This is a high honour and the REVIEW extends sincere congratulations to Dr. Wishart.

1905-09—After a long interval, word has come from Dr. E. Stanley Anderson, 580 East Town St., Columbus, Ohio.

1908-09—Henry K. Hamilton is district manager of the Manufacturers Life Insurance Company at 701 Canada Permanent Building. He was formerly manager of the Uptown Branch, 749 Yonge St.

1909-14—During the autumn the School was visited by James Eric Michael of the James Robertson Co., Montreal.

1910-17—Paul V. Moseley, we hear, is with the Muirhead Forwarding Company, Montreal.

1911-16—We are glad to hear the address of Hilliard B. Willoughby: The Canada Packers, Hull, P.Q.

1917-1918—Carl Van Winckel and his brother Edgar (1928-1929) are in business together in Linden, N.J.

1917-20—Dr. Herbert E. Pugsley is on the staff of the Muskoka Hospital for Consumptives, Sanitarium P.O., Ont. We are gld to learn Pugsley's address as it is some time since he has been touch with the School.

1919-26—Howard S. Costigane is with the Dobson Realty Co., 1454 Yonge St.

1919-26—Dr. J. D. McLennan, who has been in Port Colborne for several years, is now practising in Toronto, 696 Mount Pleasant Rd.

1922-1929—Beverley H. Black is now with the Bell Telephone Company in Montreal.

1922-30—James L. Cosgrave is with the Lake Shore Mines, and John T. W. Young ('28-32) is with the Coniarum Mines at Schumacher and played on the Timmins hockey team in 1936-37.

1923-30—John Parker and H. P. Hill ('27-'30), barristers and solicitors, have opened an office in Kirkland Lake, Ont.

1924-29—Reg B. Follett is time-keeper at the Buffalo Ankerite Mine.

1926-29—Thomas W. Barnes is with the Toronto Daily Star.

1926-29—W. G. C. Acheson (Goderich) is now with J. H. Crang and Co., Lindsay, Ont.

1927-30—H. P. Hill is in law partnership with his father in Ottawa.

1928-32—R. T. Cattle graduated from the University of Toronto in June, 1937, and is now attending the University of Nebraska.

1928-30—The REVIEW extends congratulations to John Steele Wright, who was called to the bar of the Province of Ontario in November.

"Good Old Chappie"

We have received a letter from A. G. Findley, which is quoted:

November 6, 1937.

In acceptance of "Chappie's" very kind invitation to the Old Boys' Association, the following dads and sons set out on August 20th for a Camp Kagawong week-end: Al and Jimmy Ramsay, Gord and Arthur Hewitt, Roy and Roy, Jr., MacMurtry, Claude and Peter MacMurtry, Roy and Billy Firstbrook, Paul, David and Ian Fleming, Al, Michael and Tif Findley.

In their eagerness to get to camp in time for a late swim, I understand several Old Boys had their driving licenses cancelled on charges of "low flying". On arrival the youngsters were all distributed in comfortable tents and cabins with the regular campers. The young visitors turned in with "that night before Christmas feeling" and the air fairly crackled with suppressed excitement.

The "Skipper" played host that evening to the fathers, and after the Old Boys had all talked out about the good old days at school, Chappie "took over" and gave us a wonderful talk on the value of carry-over sports.

Old Boys aboard the Hopalong, Aug. 20-23, 1937.

By noon Saturday we were all, of course, "old stagers", walking with bow-legged swaggers, and I distinctly heard Roy Firstbrook muttering orders about "boxing the centreboard" and "easing off the main deck".

Saturday evening the Senior Section opened up a perfectly equipped midway—"Hit the Nigger on the Head", "Bingo" and a haunted house complete with skeletons and ghost.

Sunday was spent in sailing, canoeing and other Camp activities, and we finally tore ourselves away in the late afternoon with a very real feeling of regret that it was all over.

The invitation and the realization were both entirely typical of "Chappie" than which nothing more superlative can be said. If the invitation is extended again, we only hope more Old Boys will take advantage of it.

(Signed)

A. G. FINDLEY

*   *   *   *

MR. KETCHUM: (to lazy new-boy)—"You will have to work harder."
NEW-BOY:—"Why?"
MR. KETCHUM (annoyed):—"Do you know who I am?"
NEW-BOY:—"No."
MR. KETCHUM:—"Well, I am the headmaster."
NEW-BOY:—"Say, that's a good job, hang on to it!"

*   *   *   *

NURSE: (to a very sick boy)—"Cheer up, my boy, the moon will soon be up."
BOY:—"Heavens! Have I to bring that up as well?"

In Montezuma's Day
Chocolate *was a favoured beverage*

LONG before Cortez set out on his first voyage of discovery, chocolate or *chocolatl*—as it was called—was the national drink of the Aztecs, their Emperor, Montezuma is said to have taken no other beverage. So highly did the Aztecs esteem chocolate that they valued the cocoa bean above gold.

Introduced by Hernando Cortez to Spain in 1526, by the end of the 17th century chocolate was *the* aristocratic beverage of Europe. It was then that chocolate houses were first established.

The best cocoa beans are grown in the equatorial zones in the West Indies, West Africa, Ceylon and other countries. Many are the processes of refinement that have been discovered since chocolate was first introduced. Because Neilson's employ the most modern machinery and use only the finest cocoa beans, Neilson's chocolate is so smooth, so rich, so delightful in flavour and matchless perfection that it is indeed the best chocolate made.

Get a bar of Neilson's Jersey Milk Chocolate, bite into it and let it melt in your mouth—truly it is—"the food of the Gods."

5¢

Neilson's
THE BEST MILK CHOCOLATE MADE

Neilson's JERSEY MILK CHOCOLATE

HS37A

Obituaries

MAJOR J. LESSLIE FERGUSSON who passed away on the 7th of October was one of the first boys to enter St. Andrew's College. He was a valued member of the first football, hockey and cricket teams and contributed much by his enthusiasm to the formation of School spirit. As one of the editors of the REVIEW he wrote a notable article on this subject which was published in the Easter number 1902. After leaving school he continued his interest in athletics, and played hockey in Nelson and Regina and football with the Argonauts in Toronto. He served in the Great War and attained the rank of major in the Army Service Corps. Lesslie Fergusson was acting secretary of the Old Boys' Association in 1909-1910, and a member of the Board of Governors 1912-1915. He was senior partner in the firm of G. Tower Fergusson Company, Stock Brokers, and a member of the Toronto Stock Exchange. The REVIEW extends sincere sympathy to his wife and family and to Mr. A. Tower Fergusson and Mr. Neil C. Fergusson, both also Andreans.

ALEXANDER WALTER McMICHAEL entered St. Andrew's in January, 1901, in the Preparatory Form and will be remembered by all the boys of that period, especially by those under Dr. Meyer's care in Rowanwood House. He remained at school till June, 1906, the end of our first year in Rosedale. After a long experience in business, he became interested in the drama and was attached to Hart House for the season of 1919-20. Next year he was with the Alexandra Theatre in Toronto. Lately Mr. McMichael, whose health had not been good, was living in Bobcaygeon where he passed away in November last. He was a loyal Andrean whose loss we lament.

MR. BRUCE McMURTY entered St. Andrew's College in September, 1915, at the age of 18, and was with the School until the following June when his studies were interrupted by the War. He served as Captain in the Mississauga Horse Cadets, a unit which passed many recruits into overseas Battalions. He served later as Lieutenant in the 116th Overseas Battalion. Invalided home he entered his father's company, The Gold Medal Furniture Company of which he became a director. Mr. McMurty was a keen horseman and for some years rode with the Eglinton Hunt Club. He was at one time secretary of the Montreal Branch of the St. Andrew's Old Boys' Association. He died suddenly on September 15th in St. Michael's Hospital. The REVIEW extends sincere sympathy to the surviving members of his family, and especially to his three brothers, Claude, Roy and Warren known to so many generations of Andreans.

YOU'LL LOVE TORONTO'S NEWEST AND FINEST MILK!

GOLDEN CREST

It's Irradiated!
It's Homogenized!
It's from Selected Herds!
It's Quality Controlled!

by

City Dairy

PHONE KI. 6151

Births

ELLSWORTH—On June 10, 1937, to Mr. and Mrs. G. Eric Ellsworth, the birth of a daughter (Sally).

DINNICK—On June 15, 1937, to Mr. and Mrs. Wilfred S. Dinnick, a son.

CAMERON—On June 22, 1937, to Mr. and Mrs. W. S. Cameron, a son.

BROOME—On August 6, 1937, to Mr. and Mrs. Edward P. Broome, a daughter.

GRANT—On August 9, 1937, to Mr. and Mrs. William J. Grant, a daughter.

ACLAND—On August 10, 1937, to Mrs. and Mr. Eric C. Acland, a son.

SAMPSON—On August 27, 1937, to Mr. and Mrs. R. Alan Sampson, a daughter.

GANONG—On September 4, 1937, to Mr. and Mrs. J. E. Ganong, Jr., a daughter.

GALLAGHER—On September 12, 1937, to Mr. and Mrs. T. H. L. Gallagher, a son.

PATTERSON—On November 3, 1937, to Mr. and Mrs. A. L. S. Patterson, a son.

Marriages

BROWNE-PERRIN—On Saturday, May 29, 1937, Kenneth W. Browne married to Miss Elizabeth Hamilton Perrin of Toronto.

TUCKER-COWAN—On Tuesday, June 1, 1937, Gilbert Norman Tucker married to Miss Frances King Cowan of Vancouver, B.C.

WILLIAMS-MCCALLUM—On Saturday, June 5, 1937, Joseph Carl Williams married to Miss Jane McCallum of Victoria, B.C.

HUME-MACDONALD—On Saturday, June 11, 1937, Frederick R. Hume married to Miss Alice Mary Macdonald of Toronto.

MONTGOMERY-DORLAND—On Saturday, June 19, 1937, A. Scott Montgomery married to Miss Mary Eleanor Dorland.

BANFIELD-STERLING—On Saturday, June 19, 1937, Edwin Arnold Banfield married to Miss Rhea Sterling of Vancouver, B.C.

YEOMANS-HOWARTH—On June 26, 1937, F. Roy B. Yeomans married to Miss Laura Howard of Halifax, N.S.

LUMBERS-MCNEILLIE—On June 26, 1937, Leonard George Lumbers married to Miss Francis Gardiner McNeillie of Toronto.

MCMURTY-GOURLAY—On June 26, 1937, William George Warren McMurty married to Miss Louise Gourlay of Toronto.

RUDDY-WILKINSON—On June 26, 1937, Robert S. Ruddy married to Miss Jessica Wilkinson of Guelph.

Buy your
PIANO, RADIO, or REFRIGERATOR
FROM
Heintzman & Company, Limited
EASY TERMS ARRANGED

195 YONGE ST., TORONTO   ELgin 6201

The

PARISIAN

LAUNDRY

Company

of

TORONTO

Limited

HARRY KENNEDY has everything in
ATHLETIC SUPPLIES

Quality goods at reasonable prices in

Canada's Finest SPORT SHOP

Special discount to St. Andrew's pupils

ADEL. 9095

Guns, Ammunition, Golf, Tennis, Baseball, and Fishing Tackle and Hockey Equipment

HARRY B. KENNEDY LIMITED

HARRY KENNEDY

113 KING STREET W., TORONTO
Open Nights

WITH THE COMPLIMENTS
of

WILSON SCIENTIFIC CO. LTD.

59 WELLINGTON ST. W. - - **TORONTO**

Telephone Elgin 6239

BREITHAUPT-ALEXANDER—On July 17; 1937, Paul Theodore Breithaupt married to Miss Jean Alexander.

MOFFAT-TILLEY—On July 17, 1937, Gordon Hamilton Moffat married to Miss Ruth Marter Tilley.

SQUIRES-LANCASTER—On August 7, 1937, Walter David Squires married to Miss Anne Lenore Lancaster of Vancouver, B.C,

FOLLETT-WRIGHT—In September, 1937, Reginald Beatty Follett married to Miss Marjorie Wright.

COSTIGANE-BRUNDRETTE—On October 9, 1937, Jack Paton Stewart Costigane married to Miss Dorothy Jean Brundrette.

THORLEY-COWAN—On October 23, 1937, Richard Gordon Thorley married to Miss Christie Isabel Cowan.

EXCHANGES

We acknowledge with great pleasure the following exchanges:

The Record—Trinity College School, Port Hope.
Junior Journal—Princeton Country Day School.
The Boar—Hillfield School, Hamilton.
The Grove Chronicle—Lakefield Preparatory School.
Stanstead College Annual—Stanstead College, Stanstead, Quebec.
The Wulfrunian—Wolverhampton.
The Canberran—Canberra Grammar School.
Trinity University Review—Trinity College, U. of T.
University of Toronto Monthly—Toronto.
The Limit—Loughborough College, Loughborough.
The Mitre—University of Bishop's College.
Voyageur—Pickering College, Newmarket.
The Harrovian—The Harrow School, Harrow, England.

COMMENTS

As Exchange Editor, I am supposed to keep our Editorial board abreast of the times and enable us to profit by the excellencies of the other school publications. I am also supposed to make an intelligent criticism of these publications. The former is easy; the latter is very difficult. Nearly all the other magazines are so excellently edited, that I suspect my remarks of possibly sounding presumptuous or patronizing. They are definitely neither. It is hoped that the magazines of other schools will tell us of our shortcomings.

Bishop's College School—Lennoxville, Quebec.—Congratulations on your Centenary number, an excellent publication. Your pictures of school life, past and present, are outstanding. You might improve your literary section.

Trafalgar Echoes—Montreal.—One of our best exchanges. Your literary section is excellent. Why not a few jokes, and a few informal pictures?

Vox Lycei—Ottawa.—A very attractive magazine; strong in all departments. We think you might scatter your team pictures more. Your jokes are excellent.

Red and Grey—Canadian Academy, Kobe, Japan.—One of our best overseas exchanges. Your literary section and arrangement set a very high standard.

J.F.M.

Whether you are on your holidays or at school the clothes you wear and the manner in which you wear them will either help or hinder you in making a proper impression on those with whom you come in contact.

In order to create the best impression it is essential that you deal with a firm that understands and caters to your needs.

BUY IT AT ELY'S

Illustrated is the type of suit that we sell and recommend for college men for their less formal occasions. Priced from $32.50.

Others from $27.50 to $45.00.

Hats   from $3.50
Shirts from 1.95
Hose   from   .55
"Ely Traveller" Overcoats from 22.50 to 45.00.

ELY'S "HARRIS" SUIT

Our prices at all times are on a competitive basis giving the first consideration to quality.

ELY LIMITED
ESTABLISHED 1902

28 KING W. — 45 BLOOR W. — ROYAL YORK HOTEL

FIRST ANGLER (Wadds):—"Yes, and I was afraid to haul it in the boat for fear I would swamp it."

ANGLER (Mitchell):—"Yea, the same thing happened to me—on the Queen Mary."

* * * *

CLERK:—"Mr. MacIntosh, how about buying the latest atlas?"

MR. MACINTOSH:—"Not now. I'll wait until the affairs in Europe are more settled."

* * * *

A little boy was saying his prayers in a very low voice.
"Speak up, son," said his mother, "I can't hear you."
"I wasn't talking to you," said the child.

* * * *

Mr. Fleming was closely examining Willis's homework.
"This looks suspiciously like your father's hand-wriring, Willis," he said. "What have you got to say?"
"Well, sir," replied Willis, after a long pause, "now that I come to think of it, I used his fountain-pen."

* * * *

"Hurry up with that game, boys," said the Aurora fire chief. "There's a fire in the next village."
"How do you know?"
"I had a post-card this morning."

* * * *

Beneath the moon he told his love,—
The colour left her cheeks,—
But on the shoulder of his coat
It showed up plain for weeks.

* * * *

A guide was showing a party of women around Niagara, when he came to the Falls.
"The scenery here is magnificent," he said, "and if the women will please be quiet we shall hear the thunderous roar of the Falls."

* * * *

DAVISON (who had just inherited a fortune):—"I'll bet you wish you were in my boots."
SHE:—"I'll say I do, especially when we're dancing."

* * * *

SISMAN:—"I'm going to leave school unless the headmaster takes back what he said to me."
MCCLELLAND:—"Why, what did he say?"
SISMAN:—"He told me to get out."

* * * *

SHE (awkward dancer):—"This dance floor is certainly slippery."
KNIGHT:—"It isn't the floor; I just had my shoes shined."

LOVE AND BENNETT LTD.
FOR
SPORTING GOODS and BICYCLES

HOCKEY BASKETBALL
SKIING BADMINTON

MAPLE LEAF GARDENS (open evenings) **TORONTO**

Branksome Hall
10 Elm Avenue, Rosedale, Toronto

A Residential and Day School for Girls

Principal: MISS EDITH M. READ, M.A.

Pass and Honour Matriculation, Art, Music, Domestic Science, Large Playgrounds, Primary School for Day Pupils. also farm of 50 acres for skiing.

For prospectus apply to the Principal

WOOD FLEMING & COMPANY
LIMITED

GENERAL INSURANCE AGENTS

PROPERTY MANAGERS

REAL ESTATE BROKERS

ELgin 6161
ROYAL BANK BUILDING
TORONTO

SHE—"What is your chief worry?"
HE—"Money."
SHE:—"I didn't know you had any."
HE—"I haven't."

* * * *

ANGUS (in the post office):—"What's the peculiar odour around here?"
CLERK:—"Probably the dead letters."

* * * *

CHRISTIE:—"While we're sitting in the moonlight, I'd like to ask you——"
ROSEMARY:—"Yes, darling?"
CHRISTIE:—"If we couldn't move over; I'm sitting on a nail."

* * * *

WAITER:—"Did you call me, sir?"
SEATON—"No; that was just the fly in my soup buzzing."

* * * *

There is one good thing about the amber light that flashes in traffic signals just before the green. It gives the Scotchmen time to start their motors.

* * * *

Two lunatics, each firm in the belief that he was a lifeguard, had escaped from an asylum and were walking along the road in search of the ocean. Presently they came upon a large wheatfield which was rippling in the breeze. Shedding their clothes they climbed a telephone pole, and the first one dived off. In a few moments his head emerged dazedly from the wheat. "Dive a little to the left," he cautioned his companion, "I struck a sandbar."

* * * *

MISS DE VIGNE:—"Now, Tommy, sit down and tell me why Mr. Ketchum caned you."
TOMMY:—"I'd rather stand up and tell you, Miss De Vigne."

* * * *

WHAT WOULD HAPPEN IF:

Mr. Laidlaw lost 'Jerry'.
Mr. J. Y. (Swing) Ross lost his pipe.
Mr. Fleming lost his little black book.
Mr. Goodman lost his glasses.
"Scoop" lost his camera.
Mr. Beer lost his Budget Book.
"Dusty" lost his swing.
McCormick lost his cat.
Christie lost 'that' picture again.
Mr. Millward lost his dictionary.
"Benny" lost his "IT."

Compliments of

Cousin's Protected Dairy Products

AURORA

BRADFORD　　　　　　　　　　TORONTO

The Provident Investment Coy.

PROPERTY MANAGEMENT

MORTGAGE LOANS　　REAL ESTATE

200 BAY STREET

ELGIN 3397 and 3398

"Sweet Brier" Sugar Cured Hams and Bacon

W. Wight & Company, Limited

60 PATON ROAD

TORONTO

COMPLIMENTS OF

DUFFERIN PAVING & CRUSHED STONE
LIMITED

FLEET ST. WEST　-　TORONTO

Special Discount to Students

BROWN'S SPORT & CYCLE
CO., LIMITED

345 YONGE ST., TORONTO

Old Boy—George L. Vivian, Jr. Wa. 2337—Open Evenings

COMPLIMENTS OF THE

T. Sisman Shoe Company
LIMITED

Aurora   **Ontario**

Compliments of

United Paper Mills Limited

Wholesale Paper Merchants
.... and Mill Agents ....

Warehouses located at

TORONTO   :-:   HAMILTON   :-:   LONDON

Compliments of

STANDARD FUEL CO.
LIMITED
K. R. MARSHALL
President

ALL FUELS

The
Panoramic
Photographers
of
Groups, Residences,
Estates, Parks, etc.

WE SPECIALIZE IN
COLLEGE and
SPORTING GROUPS

Panoramic Camera Co.
OF CANADA
289 AVENUE ROAD
MI. 3663
F. S. RICKARD, Manager
Established over 25 Years

J. F. WILLIS
Druggist - Aurora

PATRONIZE

OUR

ADVERTIZERS

The Diver Electrotype Company, Limited
110 YORK STREET   **TORONTO**

ENGRAVERS   ELECTROTYPERS

for College Men—

DACK'S
"BOND STREET" Shoes

DACK'S "Bond Street" shoes give college men the typical Dack quality which, for more than a century, has set the standard in fine footwear for men. Style—fit—comfort—durability — these combined with selected Canadian leathers and skilled craftsmanship —are factors in a value which defies comparison. See the distinctive "Bond Street" models now on display.

DACK'S
SHOES FOR MEN

73 King St. W.   Toronto

TORONTO   MONTREAL   OTTAWA   HAMILTON   LONDON
WINDSOR   WINNIPEG   REGINA   CALGARY   VANCOUVER

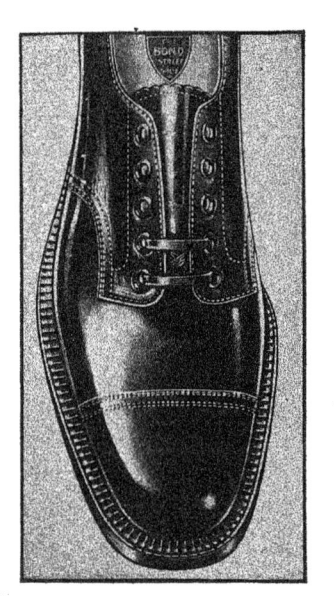

Westinghouse Mazda Lamps

AND

Magnalux Luminaire Lighting Units

FOR

BETTER LIGHT — BETTER SIGHT

H. C. Burton & Co.

Hamilton   TORONTO   Montreal

SPALDING SPORT GOODS

"The Finest Always"

HOCKEY—SKI—BADMINTON—GYM

"Latest in Sport Clothing"

TORONTO RADIO & SPORTS Ltd.

Open Evenings   241 Yonge St., TORONTO

Compliments of

BROWN BROS. LTD.

ST. LAWRENCE MARKET

ALL KINDS OF
FRESH AND SALT MEATS

| HAMS AND BACONS | Phone ELgin 7469 | POULTRY IN SEASON |

DR. E. V. UNDERHILL

DENTIST

AURORA

TRINITY COLLEGE
IN THE
UNIVERSITY OF TORONTO

Trinity College, federated with the University, is one of the Arts Colleges of the University and includes:

1. A Faculty of Arts providing instruction for students in classes of limited size in all subjects taught by the colleges.
2. The full advantages of Federation with the University, instruction by its Professors, qualification for its Scholarships and Degrees, use of its Library, Laboratories and Athletic facilities and membership in Hart House.
3. A Faculty of Divinity in which Trinity exercises its University powers of conferring degrees and prepares candidates for the ministry of the Church.
4. Residences under College regulations for men—"Trinity House"; and for women students—"St. Hilda's"; also for members of the academic staff.
5. The Scholarships offered by the College have recently been revised and largely increased. Full particulars will be supplied on request.

For information concerning Scholarships, Exhibitions, Bursaries, etc., address

The Registrar, Trinity College, Toronto 5

A Coach for the Team

Conserve the energy of your players. Let them relax at ease in a luxurious motor coach under the care of a competent and courteous driver. - -

DIRECT DOOR TO DOOR SERVICE

Moderate Rates for all Group Outings

GRAY COACH LINES
ADELAIDE 4221

ELMWOOD LODGE TEA ROOMS

Mrs. W. R. McQuade

Phone 119J   AURORA

With the Compliments of

CASSELS, SON & CO.

ESTABLISHED 1877

— *Members The Toronto Stock Exchange* —

16 JORDAN ST.   TORONTO

J. M. WALTON

INSURANCE   REAL ESTATE   CONVEYANCING

AURORA   ONTARIO

Dickie Construction Company

LIMITED

TORONTO

THE
CHINA & GLASSWARE

used in

St. Andrew's College

is supplied by

CASSIDY'S Limited

22 FRONT STREET WEST

Toronto

PATRONIZE

OUR

ADVERTIZERS

FAMED FOR FLAVOR

WONDER BREAD
— AND —
HOSTESS CAKES

Ideal Bread Co., Limited

183-193 DOVERCOURT ROAD, TORONTO

Phone—Lombard 1192

THE MARK OF A GENTLEMAN

Careful in his choice of apparel—fastidious about his letter paper. He knows that appearances count. Good writing paper is the mark of a gentleman.

Sold by all good Stationers in sizes for every occasion.

Ellis **CAMEO** *Stationery*

Made by BARBER-ELLIS of Canada Limited

St. Andrew's Colours--
RED and WHITE

You are proud of them because they stand for a fine school, with noble traditions to uphold.

Our Colours--
RED and WHITE

We are proud of them because they represent a fine group of modern well-kept Grocery Stores known for "Quality and Service".

SHOP AND SAVE AT

The RED and WHITE Stores

THERE IS ONE IN YOUR DISTRICT

AUTOGRAPHS

Canadian Securities

Dominion and Provincial
Government Bonds

Municipal Bonds

Public Utility
and
Industrial Financing

Dominion Securities Corporation Limited

TORONTO   MONTREAL   WINNIPEG   VANCOUVER   NEW YORK   LONDON, ENG.

15 King Street West, Toronto

BE UP TO DATE!

Drive a Ford V 8

TWO NEW CARS FOR 1938

DE LUXE
BIGGER
MORE STREAM-LINED
MOST COMPLETE EQUIPMENT

STANDARD
NEWLY STYLED
LARGE BAGGAGE SPACE
LOWEST IN PRICE

SEE AND DUGGAN MOTORS LTD.

621 YONGE STREET   -   TORONTO

FORD DEALERS FOR 19 YEARS

VISIT OUR TEN MINUTE CAR WASH
IRWIN AVE. (3 Blocks below Bloor between Yonge and Bay)
QUICK AND THOROUGH SERVICE—ALL MAKES OF CARS

We're "Tele"ng You— wear Grenfell Togs

'Gainst wind and weather you'll find "Grenfell" Cloth one of the toughest, most practical cloths you could wear! What's more, it should last for years.

"Grenfell" Cloth ski togs are typical of the superlative styles and quality which have made EATON'S "Prep" Clothes Shop a favourite with boys in the well-known schools as well as their parents.

The "Prep" Clothes Shop

SKETCHED
... Double-breasted jacket of "Grenfell" Cloth specially treated to withstand Labrador Winters. In eggshell colour. Other styles in maroon, royal and scarlet. Sizes 32 to 37. Each $10.95

... Ski Slacks of navy "Grenfell" Cloth half-lined with flannelette. Sizes 24" to 32" waist. Pair $9.50

Second Floor, Main Store

THE **T. EATON C**O LIMITED